A RELIGIOUS REBEL

"H.W.S."

MRS. PEARSALL SMITH

From an old Photograph

A RELIGIOUS REBEL

THE LETTERS OF "H.W.S."

(MRS. PEARSALL SMITH)

Edited by her son
LOGAN PEARSALL SMITH

With a Preface and Memoir by
ROBERT GATHORNE-HARDY

LONDON : NISBET & CO. LTD.
22 BERNERS STREET W.1

First published 1949

Made and Printed in Great Britain

PREFACE

WHEN Logan Pearsall Smith was at work on his autobiography, *Unforgotten Years*, he got out a collection of his mother's letters which had been made shortly after her death. One morning he said to me, " I've just discovered that my mother was a most remarkable and brilliant letter-writer." And from that day he resolved, some time or other, to edit and publish a selection of letters and passages from his mother's correspondence. He completed a selection, and this book is printed from the typescript he had had made of it.

It was his habit in all his works to revise extensively, even after a book or an essay was apparently completed. When he compiled his anthologies, he would get together a large collection of passages ; then, for a while, he would lose interest, and put the work on one side, taking it up from time to time, to make cuts or alterations. Not until he had been satisfied, and disillusioned, and satisfied once more, again and again, would he print his choice of extracts (there generally followed, as with his original work, a period, just after publication, of further disillusion ; the work was dust and ashes, a disgrace, and just so much time wasted ; but this always passed, and satisfaction would finally return again).

The typescript put into my hands is evidently of his first selection. He had made changes in this, and added notes to it ; but having worked with him for many years, I have no doubt at all that he would have altered this selection more than once again before publishing it. I have therefore felt justified in cutting

v

out a few passages which seemed to fall noticeably
below the rest in quality. (Little has been omitted
except early effusions of conventional piety. As will
be found in the letters, the expressions of her religion
became, towards the end of her life, more and more
personal and characteristic ; and all the original
passages revealing this have been retained.) I have
added to his choice only one extract. His own selection ends somewhat abruptly ; as a fitting conclusion
I have put in parts of the last letter sent by Hannah
Whitall Smith to her friends.

Logan Pearsall Smith, as I have said, had supplied
a few explanatory notes ; these did not appear suffi-
cient, and I have introduced a larger number of my
own. To distinguish his original ones from mine, I
have added to them his initials, L.P.S.

He had planned to write a short biographical sketch
of his mother. At one time he thought of printing
this work as the introduction to an authorised new
edition of *The Christian's Secret of a Happy Life* ; but,
unless he had made such an alteration in his style and
manner as to render them unrecognisable, his pro-
jected memoir would have been fitter as an introduction
to the more secular correspondence here published,
than to that " little religious classic ", as he refers to
it. However, by way of such a memoir, no more,
unfortunately, seems to have been achieved than the
short introduction which is printed with this book. At
the request of the publisher I have, as best I could,
filled this gap myself. My information for this work
was derived from the following sources :

1. A collection of miscellaneous material gathered
together by Logan Pearsall Smith. This consisted
largely of unpublished manuscripts of H.W.S. herself
—some early diaries, a short life of her eldest child,

Nelly, and copies of various letters which he did not include in his selection ; I have also made use of family letters from other sources. There is, too, a scrapbook full of newspaper cuttings referring to some of her public work, and that of her husband.

2. A number of her own books : *The Unselfishness of God, and how I discovered it* : *John M. Whitall, the Story of his Life* : *Frank, the Record of a Happy Life* : *Religious Fanaticism*, edited with a preface by Ray Strachey : *The Christian's Secret of a Happy Life* : *The Holy Life* (a short tract).

3. A few books by relations and friends of hers : *Unforgotten Years*, by Logan Pearsall Smith : *A Quaker Grandmother*, by Ray Strachey : *A Quaker Childhood*, by Helen Thomas Flexner, her niece : *Hannah Whitall Smith*, a small pamphlet by her friends Frances and Mary Willard.

Mention must also be made of *The American Dictionary of National Biography*, and of *Perfectionism*, by Benjamin Beckanbridge Warfield.

In addition to printed and manuscript sources, I have greatly benefited from anecdotes told me by Logan Pearsall Smith, but above all from what I have learnt in conversation with my friend, Mrs. Russell, the Alys of these letters, and last surviving child of H.W.S. ; and of her, since she will allow me to say no more, I can only record that she has given me great and indispensable assistance at every stage in the preparation of this book.

ROBERT GATHORNE-HARDY

CONTENTS

INTRODUCTION

BY LOGAN PEARSALL SMITH

THE initials *H.W.S.* were well known about seventy years ago—indeed one may almost say they became world-famous, as they were used as her pen-name by the American authoress of a little book which attained almost at once a fabulous circulation, both in America and England, and was translated into all the languages of Europe and some Oriental languages as well. After a circulation of more than a million in America alone, thousands of copies are still printed every year, and in numbers that steadily increase. In addition to this religious "best-seller", *The Christian's Secret of a Happy Life* (so the authoress named what has been described as a "little religious classic"), H.W.S. was an admirable correspondent, and a large collection of her letters has come into my hands. I believe that a selection of these will be of interest not only to those whose preoccupations are mainly religious, but to others who will enjoy reading the records of an authoress who deserves to be remembered for the vivid and witty familiar letters to her family and her friends.

H.W.S. was the pen-name of Hannah Whitall Smith, daughter of John M. Whitall, a Quaker and wealthy glass-manufacturer of Philadelphia. She was the wife, and then the widow, of Robert Pearsall Smith, whom at the age of nineteen she married in 1851. An admirable account of her life and writings will be found in the *Dictionary of American Biography* (Vol. XVII) and in the spiritual autobiography [1] which she published in 1903.   L.P.S.

[1] *The Unselfishness of God.* A charming picture of her in old age is given in *A Quaker Grandmother*, by her grandchild Ray Strachey (Revell, 1914).

MEMOIR

BY ROBERT GATHORNE-HARDY

HANNAH TATUM WHITALL, who was destined to become famous over most of Christendom as H.W.S., was born in Philadelphia, an eldest child, on February 7, 1832.

With a father and mother holding closely, as they did, to the austere and unworldly tenets of the Quakers, there might be, we could suppose, little chance of a happy childhood for their offspring. No supposition would be further from the truth. When a child of a later generation said, " It seems to me you did not do anything to amuse yourselves when you were young," she answered, " We did not need to : we had our father and mother." It was a belief of her father's, which he often proclaimed, that everybody would grow up the better for having " a happy childhood tucked under their jackets "—a precept which he carried out to the full in the case of his own children. They would—so she has recorded—race and romp and screech and scream, and climb trees, and roll down hills, and paddle, and dig in the mud ; above all, she seems to have had a fondness for making what she described as " mush-mully pies ". As she grew older, aspects of the tangible world became as fountains of ecstasy to her.

Her religious life, which she has recorded in clear and enlightening detail, may be looked on as the counter-balancing, by a splendid and triumphant common sense, of a mystical outlook that might have become unhealthy or even dangerous. During her adolescence she once prayed that her divine acceptability might be proved by the visible revelation of a ghost or an angel. She even put out a chair for the heavenly visitant to sit on.   Her failure at first dismayed her, until suddenly she realised the folly and, as she believed it, the presumptuous impiety of her attempt ; after that she never prayed again for the appearance of a spirit.

Although she grew up into a girl of remarkable beauty, she seems to have been unaware of this. However, she liked fine clothes, and knew it ; and she has recorded how her mother once bought for her daughters some shawls with long fringes, which, with careful scrupulousness, she at once cut down to a more quakerly length.   H.W.S., to the end of her life, could recall the agonies of this mutilation.

In June of 1851 she was married to Robert Pearsall Smith.   He too, came of a Quaker family, but one more intellectual than the Whitalls.   With her inexhaustible sources of maternal love, to be a mother was the proper destiny of H.W.S.   To other aspects of marriage she was not so well fitted and, until the end of her life, she never looked upon a collection of young girls without picturing them as pitiable drudges for the pleasure of selfish men (I have been told by one who knew her well, " She liked men ; but she didn't like husbands ").

It was during the early years of her married life, down to 1858, that she went through the first stages of the inward and finally triumphant struggles, which ended at last in her conversion.   During this period her first two children were born, Nelly, who died at the age of five, and Frank, who survived his childhood only to die of typhoid at the age of eighteen.   The heart-breaking death of her little girl hastened the mother's conversion.   As a consequence of this conversion, her surviving children eventually abandoned

America, to end their lives as Europeans ; and herself, to speak only of earthly things, it transported in the end to England, where she accomplished a venerable age on the banks, not of her ancestral Delaware, but of the Thames.

In 1865 her husband, who had been working with the Whitall glass business in Philadelphia, was required to move to Millville, where the factory was. She took two children with her, for a daughter Mary (afterwards Mrs. Costelloe, and then Mrs. Berenson) had been born in 1864. At Millville were born her son, Logan, and another daughter, Alys, who was to become Mrs. Russell.

She had fretted indignantly at the prospect of this unbecoming exile. Yet it was at Millville, among pious working people, and with the friendship of a Methodist milliner, that she achieved her final and complete conversion. However, the exile did not last very long. In the autumn of 1869 they were planning to move to a house in Philadelphia.

In 1862 John Whitall had established a mission for the poor in that city, and it was there that she appears to have had her first regular experience as a preacher. On the return of the Pearsall Smiths to Philadelphia she began to acquire a reputation; she had a command of easily flowing language, a not incongruous wit, and a simplicity of manner which, together, were irresistible. As a child she had had day-dreams of human glory ; when it began to touch her, she seems to have been quite unaffected by it.

At the request of a sufferer, she once, reluctantly, attempted to heal by the laying on of hands ; a cure was proclaimed. In one or two other instances she appeared to be successful (these cases were all of them, apparently, close to hysteria). After this, she tried

her powers, in vain, on a victim of cancer. Her
failure convinced her of what she had all along believed,
that she was not gifted with supernatural powers.
With no shadow of reluctance, she put aside the
reputation of a miracle worker.

In 1861, owing to a fall from horse-back, Robert
Pearsall Smith had suffered a head injury, to which
was attributed some undefined nervous affliction. In
1873 he had another attack, so severe that there was
evidently reason to fear for his sanity. To seek relief,
he travelled in that year to England. The fame of
the Pearsall Smiths, and of their doctrine, had pre-
ceded them across the Atlantic, and he soon became
associated with a preacher named Boardman, whose
teaching was very similar to theirs. In 1874 H.W.S.,
with her children, came over to England, and began to
share in his work. Her success was equal to his ; she
was everywhere adored, and because of her great
beauty, she was spoken of as " the angel of the
churches ".

Of their triumph at this time, much has been written,
and as much of its catastrophic ending. Concerning
the latter, whether its cause was an indiscretion or
something darker, no more need be said now than
that if anyone was to be blamed, it was Robert
Pearsall Smith.

Public acclaim must be sweet, even to the saintliest,
and it is hard to believe that H.W.S. felt no pangs at
all. And yet there can be found no outward evidence
of any regrets, and, in her cheerful submission, she
illustrated practically the strength and value of her
teachings. Those about her, it is true, deduced rather
than observed a feeling for her ill-fated husband which,
were not the term too strong and too decisive, might
almost have been called condescension. (In every out-

ward manner, she displayed the strongest loyalty, and he never had to suffer the slightest reproach from her.) The experience confirmed in her the belief which she always fervently preached, namely that religion should be an affair, not of the feelings, but of the will.

Sympathetic friends attempted to rehabilitate the heart-stricken man, and the woe-begone couple were persuaded to address two meetings. Their success was as great as ever ; but now they had little spirit for such work, and they would not persist in it.

The child who had planned, as H.W.S. did, a lifetime of playing, was not, as a woman, going to let any disaster interfere with her capacity for happiness. Her unfulfilled success she lay by, as I have told, without a murmur ; her religious works, although she often preached, continued most conspicuously in the writing of tracts and evangelistic books ; she gave herself up devotedly to temperance work ; and—sweetest of all labours—there was her family to rear and educate. Not only did she make certain of a happy childhood for them ; she also brought them up with a knowledge of literature that was very rare in her time and her world.

And so her life went on with little cares and hopes : worries about her husband's state of mind : news of scarlet fever at Logan's school, and the discovery, with a proud surprise, that there might be a writer and a man of letters in him : heart-breaking grief at the death of a little daughter. In 1882 her soberly-flickering orb came unexpectedly into conjunction with a very strange and flamboyant comet. Her family became acquainted with Walt Whitman, who would often come and stay in their house.

She and Whitman however, as the latter expressed it, never " hitched ". This should not, perhaps, be

B

unexpected ; and yet the old poet gravely misjudged his hostess. He took her for a prim, narrow saint, anticipating, beyond this life, a thinly-peopled heaven, together with an innumerable throng of damned souls. He was not aware that by expressing her disbelief in eternal torment, she had risked her acceptability as a preacher in England. She disapproved, it is true, of tobacco and alcohol ; but she was never, in the common meaning, a puritan. She had corrected her son Frank for not allowing himself enough happiness in his religious life. She was no lean-countenanced, thin-voiced fanatic ; to her tremendous faith, there seemed to be little substantial difference between this world and the next. She spoke of heaven in the same tone and idiom as of sublunary things. Once, when she was addressing the congregation of a Methodist church, there was a loud crash from the pulpit. " It's all right, friends," she said, picking up the infinitely sacred volume, " it's only the Bible."

While in Europe, the Smith family, all of them, had eaten of the lotus. The marriage of her eldest daughter Mary, in 1885, to an Irishman, Frank Costelloe, was the occasion for a long visit to England. Logan, now grown up, was left behind, in the slavery of the family business. His escape from that he has enter-tainingly described in *Unforgotten Years*—the father's formal resistance, with the mother's subtle and irresist-ible aid.

After that escape, the last of their native bonds were broken ; Alys, the younger daughter, remained for a while, completing her education. And then, for the rest of their lives, the whole family made their homes in Europe. They settled down first at a house called Friday's Hill, in a Sussex village ; as well, they had a house in London.

To H.W.S. the European, and above all the English, scene provided an intoxication which never altogether left her. In the adolescence of her children, middle-age had begun to weigh lightly—so far as anything could weigh—upon the gaiety of her spirit. She didn't —as she so amusingly records in her letters—she didn't at all enjoy those earlier hunting trips in the wilds, which were delightful to the rest of her family. On these occasions she found that she no longer took pleasure in wet and discomfort. No more mush-mully pies for her !

From the time of her finally settling in England, however, nothing it seemed, not even the pains and discomforts of an undignified illness, were to trouble her happiness seriously. Although she came, it is true, to long for death, this was not because it would be a release from any suffering, but quite simply as a translation to greater joys. Meanwhile, in mundane affairs, she embarked on a life with more of secular delight in it than she had ever known before—a life more innocent than innocence itself, but one which an orthodox Quaker would perhaps have looked on as too " gay ".

" As for mother," her eldest daughter was soon writing, " she's past praying for. What with the Ascot Races, the Henley Regatta, the Royal Academy Reception and the Naval Review, she has become so demoralised as to be a regular subscriber to *The Court Journal*—and, in confidence be it said, I am sure her highest, if most carefully concealed, ambition is to see her name some day among the list of the ' Élite '— ' The Duchesse de Whitall-Smith in her black velvet and the family diamonds——' "

In 1898 her husband died, unhappy, bitter, dis-appointed, his larger designs wrecked, although during

the short period of his noticeable work his influence had
been immense ; nor did it perish with his unfortunate
retirement.   Marrying, as he thought, a beautiful girl,
he had found himself linked to a giantess.   He was
sensitive and clever, and of great charm, lacking however in that integration of character which might have
enabled him to triumph, as his wife did, over their
disaster.

At about this period of her life, new vistas of delightful self-sacrifice opened up for her.   Towards the end
of the century her son-in-law, Frank Costelloe, died.
He had laid it down in his will that the children, two
daughters, should be brought up by a Roman Catholic
lady, for that was their religion.   Believing that this
arrangement might ruin the happy childhood which,
according to her father's precept, she had been so
assiduously tucking under their jackets, she contrived
to have them put under her own care, as wards in
chancery ; and she agreed to bring them up strictly as
Roman Catholics.

It is a not uncommon destiny of mothers to become
grandmothers ; to H.W.S. this condition seemed to
offer something altogether out of the ordinary ; to her
it was a divine, a transcendently marvellous relationship.

" Mother," her son had written, " has what most
philosophers have always been hunting for, a definite
logical system of moral conduct, all deduced from one
great principle, ' The children must have their fun.'
This simplifies life immensely."

" It stands to reason," she used to say, "that young
people *must* know better than we do."   Now and again,
it is true, but very rarely, the children experienced
what they called her " steam-roller manner "—a
manner known occasionally to all her acquaintances,

and through all her life—passionate and alarming out-
bursts of moral indignation. For the rest, she gave
herself up completely to her grandchildren's amusement.

Never was there so splendid or so abject an infatu-
ation. She allowed them to drag her crippled old body
up to the top of a hay-stack ; she went fifteen times
down the water-chute with them during a single afternoon ; she sat on the ice in Regent's Park, while they
skated and chilblains gathered over her feet ; she
even tried to hire an elephant for them to ride on in
the country, and only gave up this magnificent project
when she discovered that the animal would need at
least a ton of fodder daily. She was almost back to
mush-mully pies again.

Placidly, and without a struggle, she settled into old
age. She had always looked upon this world as a
place for brief abiding ; the ancient temples, when
she saw them standing up in beauty at Segesta, had
given her no humbling thoughts of mortality ; hers
was a spirit to be freed one day soon, a bird of passage,
not earth-bound as were those antique monuments.

For a few years after her husband's death she stayed
on at Friday's Hill, looking out, half amused, half
puzzled, on to the modern intellectual world as she
encountered it in the friends of her children, Bertrand
Russell, Roger Fry, Bernard Berenson, R. C. Trevelyan,
and the Sidney Webbs.

In 1904, crippled more and more by rheumatism,
until the affliction amounted almost to a paralysis, she
gave up Friday's Hill and the town house, and moved
happily into a London flat. Her grandchildren were
grown up ; she had finished with all her public work ;
and she was looking forward to death, not in any
discontent, but as to a sort of eternal holiday. "How

he must be enjoying himself today," she had written of a relative just dead.

In 1906 she moved to a house in Iffley—Court Place—which for the rest of her life she shared with her son Logan. She was happy enough there, as she humorously surveyed a world she no longer intended to trouble herself with ; she had never felt less tied to the earth, and she kept looking hopefully for evidences of approaching death. There was an alien charm, to one long come from overseas, in her very home—the Norman tower of the church, the great dark Tennysonian trees, the ever-romantic River Thames, flowing along the hem of her garden. She intended to leave it all as soon as possible, but in the meantime it was very pleasant.

To her religious followers, the old lady had become almost legendary ; and still they came to the privilege of her presence. Sometimes they made her a little impatient, and then a sort of saintly naughtiness took hold of her. Her son has told, in his *Unforgotten Years*, how she was once visited by a party of American Quaker schoolgirls. As she pondered over some appropriate words, the dark vision came into her mind of all these little girls as the slaves of overbearing husbands. " Girls," she said; " don't be too unselfish."

" Surely, mother," her son remonstrated afterwards, " when these girls go home, their pious relations will be dreadfully shocked by what thee said."

" Yes," she replied gaily, " I dare say it will make them grind their teeth."

To recount the actual process of her death, which took place in 1911, appears somehow irrelevant to her. One would prefer to think of her, as she herself playfully suggested, going off astride the tail of a comet. Weak, and often in pain, her illness prevented her from lying down, so that she had to spend the night, asleep for only a few fretful hours, sitting up in a chair. And still, as in the old days, she led the happy life she had preached and written about so often. She had given up all her work for nearly ten years ; but her faith remained with its fruits, like a pension earned and deserved, and altogether satisfactory.

A RELIGIOUS REBEL

I

A QUAKER GIRLHOOD

To her cousin, Annie Whitall

Aet. 15.

Now dear Annie, I am going to tell thee something, though I have not the least idea thee will believe it. I was out to tea the other night when someone said, that it is said that unless there is somebody within hearing thunder even would make no noise, that is, that there is no noise of any kind unless there is an ear to hear it ; I think it is the most ridiculous idea ever heard of, but they say that it is gradually gaining ground among scientific men.

Ask thy father what he thinks, I don't see how it can be possible, just suppose a house was to fall down and nobody near to hear it, according to that it would make no noise, but if someone came by in the midst it would begin to make a noise, oh ! it cannot be.

To her cousin, Annie Whitall

Aet. 18.

PHILADELPHIA, *Feb.* 17, 1850

Did thee have a good meeting ? Sarah [1] and I had very (*sic*) ; we thought Sammy Balderston was preach-

[1] Hannah Whitall's sister, Sarah Whitall, married William Nicholson, of Philadelphia, and The Lindens, Haddonfield, New Jersey. L.P.S.

ing to us when he said that silence was not worship, and that many came to meeting and sat down in silence without any thought of worship ; I verily believe that was us, for really Cousin Anne, Meeting is such a grand place to lay out plans and build air castles. Does thee ever think good ? I do sometimes positively ; I think I would love to be a minister and make very noble sacrifices and have people to admire me and almost worship me, as I do Samuel Bettle and Thomas Evans. Oh ! would it not be grand, and then I would travel all over the world, and do *so much* good. But I am only a woman, and women are so weak and dependent, and never do *any* good. There is no chance is there ? I shall have to be content to plod on in the same humdrum path, making pies and cooking and scrubbing, and mending stockings and making shirts, and feel proud if I may claim relationship with great and noble men.

Here it is nearly eleven, and I am sitting up in our study all alone, waiting for the thieves to come and steal my watch—a perfect martyr to my poor journals. I can't help thinking what a rich treat the editor of " Memorials of Hannah Whitall " will have one day.

To her cousin, Annie Whitall

Aet. 18.

1850

Thee cannot imagine, cousin Annie, what a splendid air castle I built to-day (I won't say where). I imagined that on a certain time Thomas Evans should preach to me, and all of a sudden in some unaccountable manner I should get perfectly good, just like Mme. Guyon. I should dress like mother in a cap and handkerchief, and sugar-scoop bonnet [1] and hooded cloak, and should preach at the very next meeting I attended. And oh ! what a *splendid* voice I gave to myself ; I pictured the whole meeting as almost ready to fall down and worship me, I was so magnificently eloquent, so grandly sublime.

And next I went on a religious visit to England when only 19, where the whole nation even the Queen herself crowded to hear the " young eloquent Quaker girl ", and next I went to France—but here my visions were cut short, most fortunately perhaps, or I might next have gone on a religious visit to the moon. Is it not queer, cousin Annie, but does thee know nearly all my air castles are on that subject, I have always had such an idea even from a little child that I *would* preach some day. As far back as I can remember I used to sit in meeting and look at the ministers [2] and wonder how I would feel when I sat up there and preached, as I fully expected to do : and once, at Yearly Meeting-time when it snowed, and we waited for the carriage, I tried it. I stood in Elizabeth Evans's place and imagined myself with a cap and handkerchief on and all the benches full of people, and began " my dear friends ". But I could go no further, my feelings were really awful. I was frightened and hurried down as fast as possible. Foolish, foolish child ! Of course I know now that such a thing is utterly out of the question, but I cannot help the feeling once in a while passing through my mind. I

[1] See Note I at end of Chapter.

[2] Quaker " ministers " were simply preachers. There was, of course, nothing like ordination, but merely an acknowledgement by senior members of the congregation. " This act of ' recording ' or ' acknowledging ' did not make the speakers ministers ; it was only the recognition that God had already made them such." (*The Unselfishness of God*, p. 58.)

have always said that I expected to be a minister—to be as fat as aunt Scattergood—and to be married and have 13 great children ; but don't for the world let anyone know that last expectation ;—it was the folly of my younger years, I don't expect such things now.[1]

To her parents

Aet. 18.

PHILADELPHIA, *May* 9, 1850

Depend upon it, father and mother, you have made a conquest of those Friends, and as their only resource they repay it to me. When Meeting was out I was standing near the door, when I saw Friend Anne Thornburg coming towards me and looking very pleasant. She shook my hand most cordially over and over again, and asked if she should not see me again. Oh, my dear relations, it is such a wonderful thing for me to be so much noticed by Ministers and their companions, that it really seems almost too much for me ; I don't think I should be able to bear much of it, for I should get completely above myself.

To her sister-in-law, Elizabeth Pearsall Smith [2]

Aet. 21.

ALBANY, *April* 1, 1853

Thou can never be too thankful for being a Quaker. I am sure as I sit by and listen to the ladies here, some

[1] See Note II at end of Chapter.

[2] On June 25, 1851, Hannah Whitall was married to Robert Pearsall Smith, son of John Jay Smith (1798–1883), and Rachel Pearsall, of Flushing, Long Island. From 1829 to 1851 John Jay Smith was Librarian of the Library Company of Philadelphia founded by Benjamin Franklin, and the Loganian Library founded by his great-grandfather, James Logan. (*Dictionary of American Biography*, Vol. XVII.) L.P.S.

of them old and gray, and hear how entirely their minds are filled with the perfect froth and fooleries of life, I rejoice that, silly as I am, I am preserved from being that silly. I have just been having a long conversation with a Mrs. White about whether New York or Philadelphia is the best place to buy silk. As if I, a simple Quaker, should know anything about it ! This world is a sadly foolish place. But Lizzie, let me beg of thee to wear no more Honiton lace—it is going out entirely. Nothing but Valenciennes, dearie, if thou wishes to preserve thy standing. And thy undersleeves must be cut up on the lower side in a sort of point—indeed they must, it is *so* important !

NOTE I (p. 3)

The peculiar Quaker garb was adopted, she tells us in her autobiography, as a sign of " becoming serious ", and those who received the call " would feel it their duty to appear at ' Yearly Meeting ' in the sugar-scoop bonnets, or the straight-collared coats, that were the outward sign of their inward change. . . . To ' put on a plain bonnet ', as it was expressed, seemed to me almost as much the end of all earthly human life as death would be." The awful power of this sanctified bonnet she illustrates with an anecdote from her mother's childhood : " One morning as she was crossing a lonely bridge . . . her dislike to her little ' plain bonnet ' "—her schoolfellows had laughed at her because of it—" grew so strong that she took it off and kicked it before her. All day that deed weighed heavily on her conscience, and as she came to that bridge on her return home from school in the dusk of the evening, she saw a dark shadow at a little distance up the creek. . . . She firmly believed it was the devil in person coming to snatch her to himself because of her wickedness, and, filled with terror she flew home as fast as her trembling legs would carry her, promising in her childish heart never again to rebel against her ' plain bonnet '." (*The Unselfishness of God*, pp. 103-5.)

The other garments mentioned were of equal severity. This strictness of dress was not confined to the Quakers. In her posthumous book, *Religious Fanaticism* (edited by Ray Strachey, Faber, 1928), page 203, H.W.S. tells of an old lady so pious that " she wouldn't tie a bow in her bonnet strings, but had a hook and eye to meet under her chin ". In spite of this, however, that particular old saint, having given, as she thought, almost everything to the Lord, became convinced that the Lord told her that there was one thing left to give " and that was her virginity, and that He would send a man whom she must be willing to receive in His name and surrender herself to him. She told us," H.W.S. goes on, " that she said, ' Thy will be done ', and was now awaiting the ringing of the bell and the advent of the promised man. . . . But," she adds, " whether that man ever came or not, I do not know." (See note on p. 54.)

NOTE II (p. 4)

Hannah Whitall's daydreams were sometimes of a more material character. Thus in her spiritual autobiography, *The Unselfishness of God* (published in 1903), she wrote of herself as a little girl :

" My Meetings were mostly passed in building air castles, an occupation that I felt to be very wrong, but which had an irresistible fascination for me. Curiously enough, these day dreams never took the form of love stories, as youthful air-castles so generally do, I suppose because I had never been allowed to read novels, and never heard anything about falling in love. But I always made myself out to be something very wonderful and grand, and the admired of all beholders. Sometimes I was to be a preacher whose eloquence was to surpass the eloquence of all preachers since the world began ; sometimes I was to be an inventor of more wonderful machines than had ever been invented before ; but more often I was to be the most marvellous singer the world had ever known ; and the ' meetings ' that stand out in my memory more distinctly than any others were those of one especial winter in my fourteenth year, when I endowed myself with an undreamed of gift for singing, that electrified everybody, and brought the world to my feet. Why I pitched on singing for my day dreams I cannot imagine, as it was a forbidden worldliness among the Quakers, and was something I scarcely ever heard either in public or private ; and I was myself so utterly devoid of any musical talent that during my whole life I have not been able to sing a note, or even to distinguish one tune from another. But so it was ; and there I used to sit on the bench beside my mother, through many a long meeting, outwardly a demure little Quaker, but inwardly a great prima donna (not that I called myself that), with my whole foolish little heart swelling and bursting with the glory of my triumphs on the stage, which, however, was a place I had never even so much as seen ! " L.P.S.

II

FAMILY JOYS

To her sister, Sarah Nicholson

Aet 32.

                    MILLVILLE, 1864

It is so lovely to look at my baby [1] and think of the sweet story of redeeming love that as yet she knows nothing of, which I shall have to tell her. I often whisper in her ear about the " beautiful secrets that mamma will have to tell her pet some day ".

To her sister, Sarah Nicholson

Aet. 33.

                MILLVILLE, *Mar.* 1865

Is it not awful about President Lincoln ? I actually shed tears, and feel a real weight on my heart. Whitall and Frank spend long hours discussing what awful things they would do with the murderer if they caught him, and if they were not Christians. But Bess, tender-hearted Bess, seems to think she would like to see him become a Christian.

[1] Mary Whitall Smith, born 1864, at Millville, New Jersey. Robert Pearsall Smith was appointed manager of the glass factories at Millville of Whitall, Tatum & Co., glass manufacturers, a firm founded by his father-in-law, John Whitall. L.P.S.

The baby, Mary, subsequently married Frank Costelloe, and after his death, Mr. Bernard Berenson ; she died in Italy in 1944, having lived there safely through the German Occupation.

                         7

To her mother-in-law, Rachel Pearsall Smith

Aet. 33.

MILLVILLE, *March* 17, 1865

I suppose you are plunged into sorrow on account of the terrible event that has come like a thunderbolt upon the nation. I had no idea that I felt such a deep interest in our President, or that I should have been so full of grief at his death. The future looks very dark as regards national affairs—it seems as if he must have been one of the few *indispensable* ones. However, no doubt it has all been permitted for some wise purpose, and it must be a *blessed rest* to him.

To Mrs. Anna Shipley

Aet. 34.

MILLVILLE, *Feb.* 5, 1866

It is just perfectly splendid to have two babies, and I only wish it was *three*. Mary is developing so exactly as one's fondest hopes could desire that my heart almost trembles with the weight of happiness. Logan [1] and I had our first regular battle to-day, and he came off conqueror, though I don't think he knew it. I whipped him until he was actually black and blue, and until I really *could not* whip him any more, and he never gave up one single inch. However, I hope it was a lesson to him. He is going to be another " Gorilla " over again for screaming.

[1] Logan Pearsall Smith, born Oct. 18, 1865. L.P.S.

To Mrs. Anna Shipley

Aet. 35.

MILLVILLE, *Dec.* 14, 1867

I want to know whether thy heart does not feel
drawn to have another meeting, similar to the one we
had last, for rousing up Christians to a sense of their
needs and their privileges. I confess that my soul is
burdened on account of it, and if I could I would
appoint a meeting in the Meeting House for the young,
where I might have an opportunity to speak as the
Spirit should give me utterance. I should not care
if *I* did make a fool of myself, if only the souls of
believers could be reached. I do not understand why
this burden [1] has been laid so upon *me*, who of all
others am the least able apparently to do anything in
the matter. But I cannot get from under it, nor
apparently, transfer it, and so I must simply wait on
the Lord for a way to open for any work He may
have for me to do. Now do not let me burden thee.
If thy own heart does not *freely* respond to this, let it
go and no doubt if the Lord *has* a message for me to
deliver, He will give me an opportunity.

To her sister-in-law, Elizabeth Pearsall Smith

Aet. 36.

MILLVILLE, *Jan.* 29, 1868

I am getting a black silk dress made for myself at
Proctor's in Chestnut Street. It is a very handsome
silk father gave me, and I could not bear to have it
ruined by a Millville dressmaker, so thought I would

[1] See Note I at end of Chapter.

see about having it made somewhere in town, and
stopped in at P.'s to inquire.   But they were so *frenchy*
and so overwhelmingly polite that they completely
took me by storm, and I found myself actually in their
back room being measured for a dress before I had even
so much as asked what they charged, or whether they
could make a Quaker's dress.   I came to the conclusion I was entirely too green to go to such places.

To her mother, Mary Tatum Whitall

Aet. 36.

MILLVILLE, *Mar.* 8, 1868

We begin to think we have discovered the secret of
influence over Logan, though he is without exception
the most perverse little mortal I ever encountered.
The things he loves and wants the most are generally
the things he says " No, no " to most frequently and
persistently, without the slightest provocation from
anyone thereto.   It really seems as if the fellow was
composed of two individuals, one bent on spiting the
other to the utmost of its capacity ;   and the way in
which he bites off his own nose from morning until
night, in order to spite his face, is irresistibly comical.
I never saw anything like it in man, woman or child
before.

His fondness for beautiful things is really something
quite striking.   Nothing escapes his notice, the least
little shred of bright coloured rag is carefully treasured,
and bright leaves and flowers, and above all the bright
sunset clouds seem to fill him with intense delight.   He
said yesterday as he stood looking at the latter, " I
wish they would come down here for me to see how

pink they are and I want to show them to Jesus." I should not be surprised to find him developing some artistic tastes sometime.

To her father, John Mickle Whitall

Aet. 36.

MILLVILLE, *June* 18, 1868

I had the funniest visit from the funniest Friend last week. She is an Indian doctress and came to Millville to see a patient, and there heard of our Meeting, and came up full tilt to see me. She greeted me with a hearty kiss, and expressed the greatest delight at the prospect of having a Meeting to go to, and actually proposed coming to spend 2 or 3 days in Millville to go around and try to induce people to attend the Meeting ; and seemed to think she could gather a large congregation. But I must say I feel thankful she lives 14 miles off, and that the cars do not run on First Day, and that her old pony, who thought nothing of travelling 20 or 30 miles a day, is safely sleeping under the sod, with flowers planted all over his grave ! I don't think our feeble Meeting could possibly cope with Indian doctresses !

To her mother, Mary Whitall

Aet. 36.

MILLVILLE, *Nov.* 22, 1868

I had such a curious visit the other day from an old broad-brimmed Friend, with his hair brushed straight down over his forehead. He had seen my little tract on " Early Friends ", and had found out from Smith

& English the name of the writer, and had gone to
410 Race Street with the intention of finding my place
of residence.   Robert [1] brought him out to spend the
night.   But lo ! he was a Hicksite.[2]   However, I
soon found out that he had a genuine experience in
the life of faith, and had no other trust than in the
atonement by the blood of Christ.

We rather expect " Little Rachel " will be the first
words Alys will say.   Either those, or else, " I love
Jesus ", words which Mary is continually singing, and
which somehow Alys has caught the sound of.   The
moment she can get any of us to lift her into a rocking-
chair, she begins to rock herself very vigorously and sing
at the top of her voice what sounds just like it.[3]

To her mother, Mary Whitall
Aet. 36.

MILLVILLE, *Nov.* 29, 1868

I am quite amused often as I walk through the suite
of rooms in which are deposited the various babies—
in the first one Mary and Logan—in the next little
Miss Alys, who requires a room all to herself, and in
the last madam Rachel—4 little beds— just think of it !

To Mrs. Anna Shipley
Aet. 36.

MILLVILLE, *Dec.* 2, 1868

I believe God has made me a pioneer, so that I do not
expect much sympathy or understanding as I go along ;

---

[1] Her husband, Robert Pearsall Smith.

[2] See Note II at end of Chapter.

[3] In later years the voices of Mary (Mrs. Bernard Berenson as she
became) and Alys (Mrs. Bertrand Russell) were tuned to other notes.
The fourth daughter (Rachel Pearsall Smith), born 1869, died in
1880. L.P.S.

and the breaking through of hedges, and fences, and stone walls is not a very pleasant path, I can assure thee. But it is my nature, I cannot help it ; and so I suppose must bear patiently all that befalls me in consequence thereof. I remember I was the first *private* individual in all my circle, who bought a sewing-machine, and I had to undergo absolute persecution because of it. And this is but a type of my whole life. So I suppose my Article will not be approved by any of you, and if I did not keep many of my sentiments to myself, I do expect you could hardly tolerate me.

To her mother, Mary Whitall

Aet. 37.

THE CEDARS,[1] *Mar.* 21, 1869

The fierce necessities of eating and washing clothes are like an inexorable fate ; there is no hope of evading them !—I have to tell myself over and over that it is the will of our Heavenly Father that these things should be, or I should be too much disheartened and disgusted at the fearful sensuality of it all, to give them proper and decent attention. Especially eating— that does seem so utterly useless, and yet occupies the larger part of our lives. I actually cannot enjoy my meals, my sense of the dreadful *earthliness* of it all is so great to me. I will not insist, however, that this would be the case if I had a nicely cooked fresh shad placed before me !

[1] The Cedars, Haddonfield, New Jersey, was the summer home of John M. Whitall (her father). L.P.S.

To her mother, Mary Whitall

Aet. 37.

THE CEDARS, *April* 12, 1869

Alys is one of the irrepressibles, and no mistake.
I wish you could just hear her saying " don't care ",
and see the fling she gives her little head, and take in
the full scope of the little tone of saucy independence
in which she utters it ! It is too comical for anything,
but rather fearfully suggestive. Since having her to
watch, I have come to the conclusion that some people
are born *outlaws* by nature, and that I myself was one
of these.

Dear little Logan continues to be my greatest puzzle.
He certainly was born to be an only child, for he is
always happiest when he is playing alone, and if he can
have undisputed sway in the nursery, and engross the
undivided attention of his caretakers, he is as good as
a boy can be. I find I can generally *kiss* him out of
his naughty spells, sooner than I can end them in any
other way, and I feel convinced there is a secret chord
in his nature that has not yet been touched, but that
will some day send out very sweet music.

To her son, Franklin Whitall Smith

Aet. 39.

PHILADELPHIA, *Mar.* 12, 1871

If theè *could* just be in my shoes for one day, thee
would not scold about my not writing ! My very head
seems ready to come off sometimes. I have a Bible
class every morning in the week except on 7th days,
and every afternoon a perfect levee of visitors at home.

And then no end of things to do besides. To-night I am expecting every minute Mrs. S. and Mrs. K. and Miss N. M. to tea, and then we are all to go to S. Shipley's to the Merrick Street meeting. So do forgive thy poor mother, dear boy, and comfort thyself with thinking how popular she is !

Father said something about thy having a monkey ; but don't think of it. It would plague thy very life out of thee. And they are dreadfully dirty creatures. The biggest one has already bitten me badly twice ; my hands are lame to-night from the effects of it. We have to keep them in a wooden cage, and it don't smell *very* good, and we can't half see them ; and they are a decided bother. We have now in our menagerie —two doves, two parrots, two cats, two monkeys, and four children, and it makes a lively scene when they all express their feelings at once.

To Mrs. Anna Shipley

Aet. 40.

THE CEDARS, *Aug.* 8, 1872

I want you to know how very ill Frank is. The slightest improvement was proved to be deceptive, and he is lying now very ill,—alarmingly so, it seems to me—but I know very little of this disease. His brain is the part most affected, and he is utterly prostrated. I live an hour at a time, and am kept free from all anxiety, trusting my darling boy to the Lord. I would *rather* His will should be done than anything else.

To her mother, Mary Whitall

Aet. 40.

THE CEDARS, *Aug.* 1872

It is an unspeakable mercy to be able to say from the bottom of my heart, " Thy will be done ", and to feel in truth that I would *rather* God should have had His own way with my boy, than anything else.   Much as I loved him, *I* never could have given him the peace, and rest, and joy he is in the midst of now.   I always cared more for his happiness than for my own, all his life long, and why should I not do so still.   Oh, our boy, our boy, how CAN we spare him ! [1]

To Mrs. Anna Shipley

Aet. 41.

THE CEDARS, *July* 25, 1873

The prospect is just lovely, and I am looking forward to at least three months of sweet quiet, with my baby on my lap, trotting away to the old old tune that has trotted all the others through their months of extremest helplessness and winsomeness.   I expect to receive all my friends, baby in lap, next winter, and to expound all my heresies over its poor little hapless head ; and,

[1] Frank, her eldest son, had died of typhoid at the age of eighteen. During the next year, H.W.S. wrote his life, which was privately printed.   He is pictured improvingly as a religious character who was converted when he was four years old ; but she cannot help portraying at the same time a youth of more worldly gaiety and material charm.

This gay yet spiritual character revealed itself very early in his life. When he was still a baby, his mother wrote " I was trying to make him understand about the angel in his heart . . . when he interrupted me by squeezing his little stomach very hard, and saying in all soberness, ' There, Mama, didn't thee hear the good angel squeaking ? ' "

Her life of him was afterwards published, and had a very considerable success, being translated into various foreign languages.

who knows? it may possibly be "sound" from its
earliest dawning intelligence ! !

The trouble is that no one can be induced to separate
their will from their emotions practically, and consequently cannot believe the will is working at all,
unless they feel the emotion working also. Just the
choice of the bare will alone does seem so dry and
futile, and insignificant, especially when a vast crowd
of blustering emotions oppose themselves to its action.

To Mrs. Lawrence

Aet. 41.

THE CEDARS, *Aug.* 8, 1873

Life and its utter failure has pressed upon me of late
with the most unspeakable sadness ; and I have felt
such an intense sympathy with the Lord Jesus in *His*
sympathy with the sufferings of His poor fallen world,
that I seem to have had an insight into His heart of
love beyond anything I ever knew before. It is the
anniversary of my precious Frank's release to-day.
How glad I am for him ! And now his dear grandma
too has made her escape.

It seems to me if we rightly understood the value of
things, we would weep at the *entrance* of a soul upon this
weary exile, and *rejoice* over its escape. And my poor
little expected baby with all its life to live, its burdens
to bear, its fearful risks to run, how sad for it ! How
much more blessed to have got through and to be
leaving it all behind ! The only thing that reconciles
me to its birth is, that this life is the necessary passage-
way to the life beyond, and that to reach Heaven's
rest, it must needs taste earth's weariness. But from
the bottom of my heart, I pity it.[1]

[1] The expected child died at birth. L.P.S.

To Mrs. Anna Shipley

Aet. 41.

THE CEDARS, *Aug.* 14, 1873

I cannot help feeling a deep interest in dear Anna, and this is why I presume to offer my advice unasked. Of course thee knows me well enough to know that when I give advice it is always with the understanding that I leave a perfect liberty for it to be rejected in toto, without my feeling badly. But I do want you to weigh this matter carefully. Girls have a *right* to a College education. They ought to be *made* to get it, even if it had to be done at the point of the bayonet. But since the world is not yet sufficiently advanced for that, the least parents can do is to open the door very wide to every girl who feels the least desire for it herself. I regret my own loss in this respect every day of my life, and the world has cause to regret it too ; for as I *will* be a rather public character, and will *insist* on undertaking to teach, it is a monstrous pity that I have this great lack of want of education.

You don't any of you know what I might have been, if I had had it ; I do ! So now I have said my say, and I hope to hear in a few days that Anna is going to Howland College, with a prospect of going to Vassar or Cornell or some other place afterwards, if she feels a call thereto.

To Mrs. Anna Shipley

Aet 41.

THE CEDARS, *Sept.* 10, 1873

My summer [after the death of her baby] has been a sad one, and my lookout for the future is not very bright. And I feel as if I had begun to go *down* the hill of life, and had lost all the spring and freshness. It seems to me just as though I had had my chance, and had failed, and it was all done now ; and nothing left for me but to try and help my children into a better and nobler pathway.

I wonder if that is not all we old people are meant for anyhow—just to help and guide, and guard the young ? It seems to me we are such *very* poor concerns, that we had *better* step aside and let them try their hands at it. It is painful with these aged feelings to be getting fat and young-looking, is it not ? But such is my fate. And I expect I don't *really* mean all this—only I feel so just now. I am in earnest, however, in having a profound reverence for the young, and an intense yearning to give them all the help I can.

To her sister-in-law, Elizabeth Pearsall Smith

Aet. 41.

Sept. 14, 1873

There is no earthly consideration, except being with Robert, that could make a residence in England, or even a visit there, the *least* pleasant to me.[1] And to go with a family of little children, who would necessarily in a strange land absorb *all* of my time, is not a bright prospect in any aspect of it.

NOTE I (p. 9)

The expression " burden " was often used by these Quakers with a kind of sanctified and accepted humbug. H.W.S. illustrates this with an anecdote about a preaching uncle of hers. This uncle spoke

[1] See Note III at end of Chapter.

to her brother about some holy engagements he had lately been carrying out. "As they separated, he said in a very solemn and mournful tone, 'So thou wilt see, dear James, what a heavy cross has been laid upon me.' My brother expressed his sympathy, and they parted, going different ways. But in a moment or two my uncle walked hastily back, and touching my brother on the arm said, 'I am afraid, dear James, that I conveyed a false impression in what I said about my ministry being a cross. Truth compels me to confess to thee that it is not a cross at all, but a very blessed and delightful privilege. I am afraid we preachers talk as we do about the cross in preaching, more from habit than from any reality.'" (*The Unselfishness of God*, p. 61.)

NOTE II (p. 12)

Logan Pearsall Smith, in his *Unforgotten Years*, mentions those high-minded Quaker heretics, the Hicksites; their leader, Elias Hicks, eulogised by Walt Whitman, preached a religion less formal even than the informal religion of orthodox Quakers, between whom and the Hicksites there yawned, it appears, not only a theological but a social gulf as well. "I remember," he writes, "climbing the wall that surrounded one of the Hicksite meeting-houses, and gazing in on those precincts with all the horror of one who gazes into Hell. Never since have I looked upon any object with such feelings of abomination.

"This theological horror," he goes on, "was accompanied, amongst the Orthodox at least, by an immense sense of social superiority : ours were the high places, we felt, in this world as well as the next . . . and even now, when, as sometimes happens, I meet in London Phila-delphians with the taint in their veins of Hicksite blood, I seem to know them at once, as by a kind of instinct, by a subtly mingled sense of theological and social repugnance, which I find it extremely difficult to overcome."

NOTE III (p. 19)

Just when H.W.S. was beginning to feel that her life was practically over, she was on the threshold of its greatest adventure—her appearance and great success in England when her girlish daydreams of eminence as a preacher became an astonishing reality. She and her husband during their absence from Philadelphia had learned from a little group of New Jersey Methodist working-people a life of faith and religious consecration, which they began to preach on their return to Philadelphia, and which caused great interest in Evangelical circles, not only in America but in England also. In my *Unforgotten Years* I have related how my father had been invited to England in 1873 to expound this new Gospel, and in this year he sent for his wife to bring her children and join him there. L.P.S.

III

THE FIRST CROSSING

To Mrs. Lawrence

Aet. 42.

AT SEA, JAN. 18, 1874

It seems very strange to break off so completely from my old life in this way, and to look forward to one so utterly new.   Oh how I do hope there won't be any *change* in any of you while I am away, except to grow more trusting.   Don't you grow any older any of you —tell dear sweet sister Sarah Little this too—don't get any fatter nor any thinner, nor any anything, but just let me come back and find the same old two and sixpences I left a week ago.   I cannot bear the thought of any change.

To Miss Sarah Beck

Aet. 42.

STOKE NEWINGTON, Jan. 22, 1874

Robert met us at a station a little out of London,[1] and there was a jubilant meeting : only that he looked so very Englishy, that we hardly knew him at first. He seems pretty well just now, and I do trust it will be permanent.   He is working *very* hard, and I am amazed that it does not kill him.   He seems to expect nothing else but that I will plunge into the work with

---

[1] H.W.S. and her four children settled into the furnished house at Stoke Newington, which her husband had rented for his family, and from which she wrote to an English friend.   L.P.S.

equal zeal, but I have not felt any guidance as yet in reference to it, except in the direction of the Friends.

John Taylor spoke to me to-day about giving a series of Bible Lessons in Devonshire Place Meeting House. But I told him I really could not consent to do it unless the Friends had first heard me, and were fully alive to the purport of my message. He therefore proposed, and we agreed, to invite a number of Friends to come to our house next 4th day evening to hear one of my lessons, and this evening the invitations have all been sent out. So thou must imagine me on that evening before this tribunal.

I do hope they *will* like me, for I burn to see this glorious life of faith becoming once more the realised experience of my dearly loved Society. But if they do not like me, then I shall know God has not chosen *me* to help in the great work among Friends here, and shall be perfectly content. My heart does yearn over Friends so.

Feb. 7, 1874

My meeting here last 4th day evening passed off quite satisfactorily, I think, and yesterday the Friends met for the purpose of deciding whether to invite me to give them a series of Bible readings. A note from J. Taylor this morning says they were unanimous in wishing it, and he is to come this evening to tell me about the arrangements.[1]

To Miss Sarah Beck
Aet. 42.

March 25, 1874

I am going to-day by appointment to meet the Duchess of Sutherland, at a Lady Ashburton's ; and

[1] See Note I at end of Chapter.

then to lunch with Lady Gainsborough, and I must
hasten off to get ready.

To Mrs. Henry Ford Barclay [1]
Aet. 42.

VENTNOR, *June* 5, 1874

Whenever I think of you, I always think at the same
time of an old legend of a lovely lady, upon whose
house the sunshine always rested, even when all was
storm and darkness around.   The fame of this reached
the ears of the Bishop, who went to see her that he
might discover by what austerities or self-denials she
had gained such wondrous favour.   But he found that
they all came from the utter simplicity and childlike-
ness of her faith, and that her life had no austerities in
it, but only great love.

To her husband, Robert Pearsall Smith
Aet. 43.

PHILADELPHIA, *April* 27, 1875

I cannot *ever again* go into any English household,
and ask their servants to lift our heavy American
trunks.

I do not suppose they will think a woman's book
worth attacking, but in case they might, thee had
better wash thy hands of it at once by proclaiming
everywhere what an irrepressible wife thee has, who
will say her say in her own way, and cannot be tamed.
For I shall not alter a line to please anybody.   Every
line I write is a *pure favour* to the world, and I ask no
favours from anybody. [2]

[1] One of the Gurneys ; she had married the brewer, who lived at
Monkhams, in Essex.
[2] She was referring, of course, to her most famous book, *The Christian's
Secret of a Happy Life.*

The separation from thee is very hard, but if it is right for thee to go, we must try and bear it cheerfully, for I am *sure* it is not right for me to go around with thee, now while the children need me so constantly. We shall have to take up our cross in the matter of being separated, if thee *must* go.

I notice what thee says about not going back into business again, but have not said anything about it. I cannot advise. I suppose the Lord will care for us, if thee really feels it thy duty ; but indeed, my darling husband, I cannot consent to live on other people. I am sure it would not be right. I can go and live over at the Barracks and economise, or I can go to work to gain our living myself. But I *cannot* " sponge ", or live on collections or subscriptions. PLEASE do not ask me to do this. I can see plainly that the Lord is calling *thee* to a life of devotion to His service, and I rejoice in it. But I am sure it can be managed without our living on other people.

To her parents, John and Mary Whitall

Aet. 43.

MONKHAMS, ESSEX, *May* 26, 1875

At eleven we took the express train from Liverpool for London, with 27 articles of luggage, none of which, however, I am thankful to say, were very large. It is the English fashion to travel with any amount of boxes, bandboxes, and bundles, and bags, but no heavy trunks, and while it is bothersome to the owner, it is far more merciful to the porters, and I fully approve of it.

The worst of it is having no checks, and the necessity one is under of running after your luggage and looking it up at every change of train. When we got to

Willesden, the station at London where we were to meet Robert and change cars for Dalston, Robert and I just had to rush, without even exchanging a kiss, to hunt up the luggage, and did not dare to take time even to contemplate one another's countenances until it was all safely deposited in a small pyramid on the platform.

I could introduce some improvements into their railway arrangements here, if they would only consult *me* ! A very flagrant need of their travelling routes is *water*. I went into a restaurant that was in the Depot and said to the woman there very mildly, " Can you tell me where I can get a drink of water ? " She was surrounded with bottles of wine, but no sign or token was to be seen of any other drink. She looked at me in perfect amazement, and exclaimed in a tone of wonder, " Water ! ? " " Yes," I replied, " water, water to drink." " I suppose you can get it somewhere outside," she said much in the same way as she might have said, " She supposed there *were* unicorns somewhere in the world, although she did not know where." I do confess I felt like explaining matters to her with a little American enthusiasm.

We then tried the railway porters, who were standing about, and they said in the same dazed sort of way that they supposed there was some in the restaurant. But we explained that we had tried there without success. They consulted together and seemed utterly perplexed, but finally one man brightened up, as though he had at last hit it, and beckoned to us to follow him. We obeyed, and after going down quite a flight of stairs to an underground platform, he unlocked a private room, and there triumphantly showed us a hydrant, with a broken glass goblet beside it. We hailed it with joy, as you may imagine.

D

Robert really seems very well, in spite of his heavy work, and the accounts he gives of the work on the Continent are even more marvellous than the letters were. It really seems as if the whole German and Swiss Churches were moved to their very centre by his message of a full and a present salvation. Hundreds are being converted just by the singing of that hymn " Jesus erretet mich jetzt ". Such is the enthusiasm that an order has come to a London photographer for 2000 of Robert's pictures, and the photographer has made so much money that he actually gave Robert £50—nearly $300.00—to sit again. A new way of making money, is it not ? And now it is evening, and Robert's one holiday has come to an end. To-morrow morning we go in to Mr. Cowper Temple's to breakfast with Gladstone, who is coming there on purpose to meet Robert and have a talk with him.

[LATER]

This morning we went to Friends' Meeting. It was a very large meeting, and quite an interesting one. Edward Backhouse gave a *ringing* testimony to full salvation, that did my very soul good. His wife told me afterwards that she could hardly help laughing at the delighted expression of my face. Charles Braithwaite and I kept nodding at one another all the while, across the meeting. Edward Backhouse has come to attend the Conference, and so had Isaac Brown, who also spoke beautifully. " H.W.S.", the irrepressible, must also needs have her say. And behold, I found afterward that I had been preaching to John Bright and his wife and daughters. Mr. Cowper Temple introduced me to them after meeting, and I had quite a little talk.

So now I have seen both Gladstone and Bright,

England's two great statesmen. I must tell you one thing that Bright said to Mr. Cowper Temple about my speaking—that I was one of the few people who could preserve a natural conversational manner *on their legs*. I think myself, to preserve it in Friends' meeting was quite as much. But then I do feel so at home with all the dear Friends here, and they do make me so welcome, that I hardly could help being natural.

To her parents

Aet. 43.

MONKHAMS, WOODFORD, *June* 13, 1875

Robert has had another £100 given him on account of the sale of his picture. Eight thousand have been sent for from Germany ! . . . I have the prospect of this nice time of rest . . . but I am only afraid the dear Swiss friends who were at Brighton will find me out, and *make* me hold meetings. I have actually been thinking of disguising myself in a fashionable bonnet to avoid discovery, and Mrs. Cowper Temple proposed lending me one.

NOTE I (p. 22)

She does not mention in her letters the awkward—indeed the critical—incident at this meeting, which very nearly ruined her Evangelical prospects in England ; Lady Mount Temple (then Mrs. Cowper Temple) has recorded it in her Life of Lord Mount Temple : " Hannah was sitting in a little circle of excellent orthodox friends, who had assembled to hear some of the good things that she had to impart, and she was there on examination.

" She happened to have seen a funeral in the street, and as she spoke of it, we all put on the conventional look of sadness. ' Oh,' she said, ' when I meet a funeral I always give thanks for the brother or sister delivered from the trials and pains of this mortal state.' How wonderful, I thought, and I could not help exclaiming, ' Is that possible ? Do you feel this about everybody ? ' I was indeed an *enfant terrible*. She stopped a moment and looked around. She was amongst a party of evangelicals, at a time when the universal hope was deemed a heresy, and she was on her trial. She owns that she went through a few moments of conflict. But truth prevailed, and looking up, with her bright glance, she said, 'Yes, about everybody, for I trust in the love of God.' I yielded my heart at once to this manifestation of trust and love and candour."

Logan Pearsall Smith, in *Unforgotten Years*, has described this event somewhat differently ; his mother, he says, had already been suspected of views not altogether sound on the matter of eternal torment. Her husband and her friends, who were in the know, advised circumspection, and " she had agreed that it would be wiser to give evasive answers on this point ", but, when the delicate moment came, " she could not, she avowed to the assembled company, believe that the God she worshipped as a God of love was capable of such awful cruelty ; sinners, of course, He punished, but that He had decreed that their torments should be unending was to her a horrible belief. Her audience were inexpressibly dismayed by this declaration ; the myrtle, in Keats's phrase ' sickened in a thousand wreaths ' ; the company was on the point of breaking up in confusion when from the depths of that great drawing-room there floated forward, swathed in rich Victorian draperies and laces, a tall and stately lady, who kissed my mother, and said, ' My dear, I don't believe it either.' This lady, of course, was Mrs. Cowper Temple." He adds that but for this spectacular intervention, his parents might never have taken to preaching in England, " and the ties and friendships which drew us all back again to England would never have been formed ". For—or so he implies—it was the worldly greatness of her new friend which saved H.W.S. from the consequences of her heresy.

Logan Pearsall Smith, it must be admitted, possessed a picturesque and sometimes imaginative memory ; but it may be that Lady Mount Temple over-decorously softened, in her telling of it, this momentous incident.

Lady Mount Temple was a Tollemache, and was the second wife of Lord Mount Temple (his first wife had been a Gurney). As well as being a hospitable leader of the evangelicals (Broadlands became almost a second home to the Pearsall Smiths), and a politician of advanced and high-minded views, he was a patron of the arts. Rossetti used to stay at his house ; Christina Rossetti was invited there ; and, as a friend of Ruskin's, he was an original trustee of the Guild of St. George.

The religious conferences at Broadlands, where H.W.S. often preached, became famous. Logan Pearsall Smith collected some descriptions of these from obituary notices of Lady Mount Temple ; the house, it is said, was filled to the attics and many of the guests overflowed into the inns of Romsey. Famous people attended, in the company of others less famous, and among the orators there had been noticed " a Jew who had been converted by studying the Law of Sacrifice, a negress who had been a slave, and a working printer who taught that sin was a disease ".

IV

BACK IN THE STATES

To her parents

Aet. 43.

The descent into the valley of the Leuch was so steep that there was a continual danger of getting into a run, in which case no earthly power could have saved me from dashing right over the edge at the next sharp turn. It was really a *frightful* walk. I can assure you the flat sandy roads of Jersey looked beautiful and lovely to my mental vision, and I feel as if all my life long I had treated them with the most cruel injustice in not appreciating their charming flatness. Never again shall I sigh for mountains or valleys in the country of my habitation.

To her parents

Aet. 43.

BALTIMORE, *Oct.* 18, 1875

We three sisters do enjoy so intensely being together. We stick close together, and are quite the admiration of the Meeting, for our wonderful likeness to each other, and the love and unity that manifestly exists between us. Aunt Julia said it was such a comfort on First Day, when poor dear Friends were screaming out their sermons, to look down at us three, and know how we sympathised.

To Mrs. Henry Ford Barclay

Aet. 44.

THE CEDARS, *June* 3, 1876

It is just a year since the great Brighton meeting, and the contrast between our lives then and now is certainly a very mysterious one.   Personally I greatly prefer the utter quiet and seclusion of the present, but it makes my heart ache to look at my dear husband, and think of the blight that has fallen on him.[1]   You think I make a mistake to say that his life is blasted. You would not say this if you knew him, or if you could at all appreciate the crushing blow that has fallen upon him.   A more sensitive, tender-hearted, generous man never lived, and this blow has sorely crushed him in every tender spot.   It would have been so impossible for *him* to have treated anyone, even an enemy, as he has been treated by those who professed to be his dearest friends, that it has utterly crushed all power from his nature of trusting anyone, and he has shut himself up from everyone.

Then in a thousand ways, which no one knows but ourselves and those who have thus trodden down a tender trusting spirit, he has been wounded past healing.   He often says to me that his life is one long agony from morning until night, and from night until morning, in every working moment.   It could not possibly be otherwise ; and I have not the faintest hope that he will ever recover from it.

There *are* storms which uproot and overturn even the stateliest trees, and what wonder then if the weaker ones are utterly prostrated by them.   *Such* a storm has swept over us, and has left only a few broken and

[1] See Note I at end of Chapter.

withering branches. The *song* has gone out of our lives, and only patient and cheerful endurance is left. We are content, however, that it should be so, since it is the will of God, and have no thoughts in our hearts of anything but loving submission to Him. While we *thought* He wanted us, we gave the very best we had without stint or measure, but this is all over now.

We have come to our country home for 5 months. We absolutely decline all the urgent requests to hold meetings etc. that come to us continually, and go nowhere. I sit mostly from morning until night in a little bay window that overlooks the children's croquet ground, and from where I can just see the dear parents' home across the lawn through the trees. It would be impossible for *you* to conceive of such a quiet secluded life, and I expect it would not seem pleasant to you, but if you had had such a heart-scald as *we* have, you would understand how thankful we are for such a refuge.

But I did not mean to write in this strain, for I have no feeling of complaining in my heart. My life is full of the dear children's interests, and of sweet cares for my husband and parents. A *commonplace* life is I am sure by far the most desirable life for a woman, and henceforth I shall seek to make mine such most emphatically.

Our children are having a happy summer. Mary and Logan have both been to a swimming school and have learned to swim, and there are several small lakes and streams near us where they can swim. They have a boat and a horse, and, more than all, the liberty of American children, which means more than you can imagine. They have just come up from a paddling excursion in the woods, where they have been revelling in mud and water, and all sorts of fun.

To Mrs. Anna Shipley

Aet. 44.

THE CEDARS, *Aug.* 8, 1876

Now I am going to give thee a plain unvarnished statement of *facts*, and thee may make what theory out of them thee pleases. I confess I am utterly nonplussed and cannot make any. First of all as to the plan and object of the meeting. It was planned by Dr. Cullis and its sole object was to reinstate Robert in the eyes of the church and the world. I always said it ought not to have been called a " Convention for the promotion of holiness ", but a " Convention for the promotion of Pearsall Smith ".

Neither Robert nor I approved of it nor wanted it held, but Dr. Cullis was so sure it was " of the Lord ", and had so set his heart on it, that, as he had stood by Robert more nobly and grandly than any other human being, we both felt constrained simply out of gratitude to him, to yield to his wishes.[1] To be fairly honest about it, we neither of us felt for a moment as if we were serving the Lord in the matter at all. We both have felt ourselves dismissed from *His* service for a year now ; but we hitched ourselves on to Dr. Cullis's team, and concluded the Lord would not be very angry with us under the circumstances, though I confess I often secretly thought it would serve us right if He should make the meeting a complete failure as far as Robert and I were concerned. And to tell the truth I did not care whether He did or not. I only want

[1] Of this convention Logan Pearsall Smith wrote, in *Unforgotten Years*, "Neither my father nor mother wanted this ' Scamp Meeting ', as Dr. Cullis wittily called it, but he said ' it was of the Lord ', and forced them to attend it."

Dr. Cullis's joke depended on the fact that at this time Camp Meetings were a regular feature of religious life in America.

the will of God done under all circumstances, and I really don't much care what His will is.

I felt utterly indifferent to the meeting in every way, except that it was a great trial to me to leave my home and the sweet children. Nothing ever made Christian work pleasant to me except the thought that I was doing the will of God, and now that that is gone, I find *no* pleasure in it whatever. So we made no preparations for the meeting, we neither studied, nor prayed, nor meditated, nor in fact thought about it at all. We had got it to do, and when the time came we meant to do our best, and the rest was in the Lord's hands. We both of us hated it cordially, and felt we should be only too thankful when it was over.

It was in no sense a religious or " pious " undertaking on our parts. We were neither fervent, nor prayerful, nor concerned, nor anything that we ought to have been. Thou sees I am telling the *honest* truth. And I really cannot imagine a meeting begun in a worse frame of mind that ours was, according to all one's preconceived notions of what is the right and suitable thing. And in precisely the same frame of mind we went through the meeting. It was all a wearisome *performance* to us. We did it as over an impassable gulf. The flood had come since the last time, and changed all things to us. There was no interest, no enthusiasm. The meetings were a bore, the work was like a treadmill. We counted the hours until we could get away, and hailed the moment of emancipation with unspeakable joy. And all pious chroniclers or church historians would have been compelled by the force of their logic to have added to this record, " and no wonder the meeting was an utter failure ".

But still, to keep to *facts*, I am compelled to record that the meeting was a *perfect success*. There was just the same power and blessing as at Oxford or Brighton, only on a smaller scale, because of the meeting being smaller. There was every sign of the continual presence of the Spirit. Souls were converted, backsliders restored, Christians sanctified, and all present seemed to receive definite blessings. It is said by Dr. Cullis, and *to* him by many others, to have been the best meeting ever held in this country. And it really *was* a good meeting, even I, uninterested as I was, could see that. There was just the same apparent *wave* of blessing as swept over our English meetings. And Robert and I never worked more effectually. He had all his old power in preaching and leading meetings and the very self-same *atmosphere* of the Spirit was with him as used to be in England. As for me, thee knows I am not much given to tell of my own successes, but in this case in order that thee may have all the *facts*, I shall have to tell thee that I was decidedly " favoured" as Friends say. In fact I don't believe I ever was as good. All who had heard me before said so.

The fuss that was made over me was a little more then even in England. The preachers fairly sat at my feet, figuratively speaking, and *constantly* there kept coming to me testimonies of definite blessing received while I spoke. The second time I spoke a Democratic [1] Editor was converted and consecrated on the spot ; and I could scarcely get a minute to myself for the enquirers who fairly overwhelmed me.

I hate to write all this, and thee must tear it right up, but how could thee know it unless I told thee, and the facts thee must have in order to see what a muddle it all is. For who would have *dreamed* of such an outcome to the indifference and want of every sort of proper qualification for their work, which I have

[1] This, of course, refers to the political party of the convert.

described beforehand? I must say, it completely upsets all *my* preconceived notions, and I do not know what to make of it. They all talked to me most solemnly about how dreadful it was in me to *think* of giving up public work, but I was utterly unmoved, and both Robert and I came away more confirmed than ever in our feelings of entire relief from everything of the kind. *We are done!* Somebody else may do it now.

The one satisfaction of the meeting to *us* was this, and it *was* a satisfaction, that Robert was treated with all the old deference and respect. . . . Henceforth home and home life for us. To be a " good house-keeper " seems to me the height of honour now ! We had to refuse lots of urgent invitations to hold meetings in various places, but we did it without a longing thought, only *too* thankful to be released.

And now, WHAT does thee think of it all ? *I* think one of two things, but which one I think I don't know. Perhaps thee can tell me. Either I was awfully wicked in the whole matter, and God was not in it anywhere, and all the success was by force of natural gifts and talents. Or else I was awfully good, so good as to have lost sight of self to such a degree as to be only a straw wafted on the wind of the Spirit, and so consecrated as not to be able to form a desire even, except that the will of God might be fully done.

I waver about myself continually. Sometimes I feel sure I have progressed wonderfully, and that my present sphynx-like calm and indifference to every-thing whether inward or outward except the will of God, is very grand. And then again I think I am an utterly irreligious and lazy fatalist, with not a spark of the divine in me. I do wish I could find out *which* I am. But at all events my *orthodoxy* has fled to the winds.

I am Broad, Broader, Broadest! So broad that I believe everything is good, or has a germ of good in it, and " nothing to be refused ", if it be received with thankfulness.

I agree with everybody, and always think it likely everybody's " view " is better than my own. I hold all sorts of heresies, and feel myself to have got out into a limitless ocean of the love of God that overflows all things. My theology is complete, if you but grant me an omnipotent and just Creator I need nothing more. All the tempests in the various religious tea-pots around me do seem so far off, so young, so green, so petty! I know I *was* there once, it must have been ages ago, and it seems impossible. " God is love ", comprises my whole system of ethics. And, as thou says, it seems to take in *all*. There is certainly a very grave defect in any doctrine that universally makes its holders narrow and uncharitable, and this is always the case with strict so-called orthodoxy. Whereas, as soon as Christian love comes in, the bounds widen infinitely. I find that every soul that has travelled on this highway of holiness for any length of time, has invariably cut loose from its old moorings. I bring out my heresies to such, expecting reproof, when lo! I find sympathy. We are " out on the ocean sailing ", that is certain. And if it is the ocean of God's love, as I believe, it is grand.

But enough! Now what will thee do with it all? " Be not righteous overmuch " is a salutary check I think. But oh how sad, that the nearer we seek to approach our God, and the more we try to please Him, the greater our dangers! That is, not *sad*, since it is His arrangement, but very perplexing. I guess He means us to be good *human beings* in this world, and nothing more.

To Mrs. Henry Ford Barclay

Aet. 44.

PHILADELPHIA, *Dec.* 16, 1876

Old age is so very sad I think, after active and useful lives, and it is not often anything but a burden. But since it is the will of God so many should have to endure it, there must be some good end in view, and we shall know all about it sometime. My dear aged parents are about as usual. They are able to go out daily, but are feeble and delicate, and need most tender care and attention. My time continues to be almost wholly occupied in waiting on them, and it is the sweetest occupation I could have.

My father is one of the executors of a large estate, and he goes down town daily to attend to it. I wait on him there right after breakfast, when I have seen the children all off to school, and then go for him in an hour or two. In the afternoons we very commonly drive in our beautiful city Park, and Mary goes with us on horseback whenever the weather is suitable. In the evenings, after the children are through with preparing their lessons for the next day's school, and have all gone to bed, I go in and read aloud to my parents for an hour or two. And so the day is pretty full without going outside of my dear home circle.

To Mrs. Henry Ford Barclay

Aet. 45.

PHILADELPHIA, *April* 13, 1877

Friends here are enjoying Stanley Pumphrey exceedingly ; I mean those we call *Gurneyite* Friends. Among the others he is most unwelcome because of the turn-down collar of his coat, and they can hardly endure to see him in their galleries.[1] Only this week he attended the Quarterly meeting at Haddonfield, which is the meeting we attend when living at our country place, and as he was going in the door, a Friend met him and told him that the Elders had met and had decided to request him not to sit facing the meeting on account of his coat ! So he had to betake himself to the side benches. Can thee imagine such darkness in this century, and only 6 miles from Philadelphia ? And even in this city in two or three of the meetings they only permit him in the gallery on sufferance, because some of the Gurney friends actually force him up there, and they neither rise, nor bow their heads, nor take off their hats when he prays, I believe some of them put them on and jam them down as a testimony against him ! I do not think he minds it much however.

I must tell thee such a smart thing about Ray [aged 8]. The other night when I was just leaving her after her goodnight kiss in bed, she said in such an old fashioned way, " Well mother, I have had my first doubt." " Thy first doubt," I exclaimed, " why what was it ? " " Why," she answered, " Satan came to me and said, ' Ray, thee must not believe that Jesus loves thee, for he don't. ' " " Well," I asked, " what did thee say ? " " Say," she repeated enthusiastically,

---

[1] As I have already noted, the clothes of the men—as well as the women's—were an almost necessary token of holiness. I do not know if this particular English Friend wore a beard ; for, to the Philadelphia Quakers at least, beardlessness was also needful. It was perhaps an earlier English Friend of whom H.W.S. wrote (for she seems broad-mindedly to have swallowed the get-up of Stanley Pumphrey), " In spite of the fact that I have a great reverence for English Friends, his beard seemed to me so evidently the mark of the evil one, that I felt it almost a sin to listen to his preaching. In several ' strict ' Meetings this same preacher was refused entrance to the ' gallery ' because of his beard." (*The Unselfishness of God*, p. 134.)

" why I just said, ' Satan I will believe it,' and then he went away." I was delighted to find how clearly she understood the right way of dealing with doubts, and encouraged her in it.

The next evening she had still further attacks to report ; " Well mother," she said as I was tucking her up in bed, " Satan has been at it again." " And what did he say this time ? " I asked. " Oh," she replied, " he said, ' Ray, if I was thee I would not believe the Bible is true, for it is not,' and he tried to coax me not to believe it." " And what was thy answer ? " I asked. " Why mother," she replied, " I just said to him ' *Satan* shut thy mouth ! ' " The emphasis with which she repeated this sentence was fairly laughable, and yet thee may imagine how thankful I was to find how well she understood it all.

She has been cured by Dr. Cullis's prayer of faith of a longstanding and very suffering dyspepsia. She went through quite a little conflict before she could come to the point of letting him pray and lay hands on her, but finally gave up and trusted, and has been perfectly well now for more than a month. She said to me the next morning, " Mother, Satan makes it very hard for me to believe that I am healed," but with this exception her faith does not seem to have wavered, and the cure is complete.

To Miss Priscilla Mounsey [1]

Aet. 46.

PHILADELPHIA, *April* 10, 1878

Dear friend, I have felt inclined to give thee a word of admonition, in noticing the recurrence again of thy old trouble of self-analysis and self-reflection. Thy

[1] An English spinster and devout friend. L.P.S.

inward dryness and barrenness, which so often trouble thee, are simply after all moods of feeling that may arise from a thousand surrounding causes of health, or weather, or good or bad news of outward things ; and they have no more to do with the *real* attitude of thy soul toward God, than a headache does, or a fit of indigestion.

To her husband, Robert Pearsall Smith
Aet. 46.

PHILADELPHIA, *April* 19, 1878

My own darling husband. This morning a plain Friend came to see me who thinks she committed the unpardonable sin when she was a little girl at Boarding school, and is almost crazy with agony ! I just pooh-poohed the whole thing of course, and *made* her begin to say " Jesus saves me." One of her troubles is that she has felt for a long time as if she ought to pray for her husband and has never done it. I made her promise to do it tonight when she went home.

E. C. Gibbons was here yesterday. She says Mr. McVicker was delighted at the plainness with which I declared Restitution [1] at Israel Maule's funeral, and I believe rather wondered I was not afraid, but of what should I be afraid ? If I hold an opinion I would far rather people should know it. And I confess if it makes people afraid of me, and anxious *not* to have me at meetings and things, I shall be only too glad. Anna Crew told E. Comstock that my friends were praying for me, that I might be brought back from my sad unbelief ! I have not a minute more, except to add warmest and tenderest love.

[1] By " Restitution " she means her quite heretical belief that damned souls will eventually be rescued from Hell.

To Mrs. Anna Shipley

Aet. 46.

THE CEDARS, *June* 15, 1878

As to " ups and downs ", beloved, don't thee know that I am one of the kind who never have any ? My path seems to lie along a sort of *dead level* arrangement, that is very comfortable, but not at all glorious. My whole experience seems to be hopelessly commonplace always, except when I come in the way of fanatics, if they are fanatics. And even then the glamour of the fanaticism *will not* get into my life, do what I may. I see its heights, but cannot scale them, and have to trudge on in the homely old ways, like a poor stupid ox. I cannot even get any inward voices and never could. I remember when Anna Richards [1] was in the depth of her mysticism, I tried hard to walk in the same paths, but in vain. Scruples *would not* come, although I tried to cultivate them assiduously. I even wooed a sugar scoop " concern ",[2] and caps and hand-kerchiefs, but it was all of no use. And just so it seems to be now. With the exception of that affair of novel-reading I do not find myself " called " into anything nor out of anything. Even my Christian work comes to me in commonplace ways, and with none of the romance of Quaker " concerns ". I expect the poetry

---

[1] The wife of an American painter, well-known at this time.

[2] A " concern " was the name given to those inward impulses which were looked upon as the irrefutable and secret instructions of the Lord. " A Quaker ' concern ' was to my mind clothed with even more authority than the Bible, for the Bible was God's voice of long ago, while the ' concern ' was His voice at the present moment, and, as such, was of far greater present importance." To the feminist in H.W.S. these voices were a matter for congratulation, since, as she writes, " not the most tyrannical ' man Friend ', even if he wanted to, would ever dare to curtail the liberty of his womenkind, if only they could say they ' felt a concern ' for any course of action '. (*The Unselfishness of God*, p. 82.)

of mysticism is not for me, and I have got to plod on in
the prose of commonplace life always.

Journal Letter to her friends [1]

Aet. 46.

THE ADIRONDACKS, *July* 22, 1878

Night before last there came up a violent thunderstorm just at bed-time, most unexpectedly, and we had
everything lying around, and *such* a hustling time as
we had !   There were 2 or 3 parties out in boats, and
I had made up a great big camp fire on the rocks to
guide them home, and when the wind blew up it began
to blow the sparks all over the dry grass and towards
the tents.   There were several fires already burning
in the mountains, and I was afraid we should soon have
one in our camp if prompt measures were not taken,
so I had to scatter the burning brands as fast as possible
down the rocks into the water below.   Then having no
possible light except matches there was no hope of
finding anything, and we just had to grapple our way
through, regardless of every consideration of comfort
or propriety.

At last we got settled in our tents comfortably, when
Mary felt her pillow heave up and down as though some
live creature underneath were trying to make its way
out.   We *thought* it was a snake, and I had to march out
in the dark and the rain through bush and briar to call
one of the guides out of their birch bark shanty to come
and catch the thing.   So much for the outward.   And
now for the inward.   How do I like this sort of life ?
I do not like it at all.   I can't sleep comfortably any-

---

[1] A number of such letters " to her friends " will appear in this book.
Her custom was to send a letter to a particular correspondent, enclosing
a list of other friends—sometimes as many as from fifteen to twenty—
among whom it was to be circulated.

where off of a spring bed with good bolsters and pillows. Moreover four thick (Mary, Alys,[1] Ray and myself) in a bed is rather too much, even although I have had Alys fenced off with stakes. Then I cannot eat in a muss, nor do I like to get along without bread. I do not care for boating, nor fishing, nor hunting, and sitting on a log does become monotonous after a while.

July 23, 1878

We beached our boats on a sandy beach in the midst of water lilies and began a wild mountain climb, finding our path only by the " blazes " on the trees. It was a beautiful walk, or climb rather, and my spirit enjoyed it greatly, but my poor old fat body refused to respond to the spirit within, and I was soon suffering such agonies of fatigue from the climbing that I believe if I had had the prospect of a view of the whole universe from the mountain's top I could not have been induced to ascend it. I got half way up, and then gave out utterly. This has settled forever my climbing of mountains. I have passed the age when it is possible, and I may as well accept the fact at once. Hereafter I shall sit, and the rest may climb.

July 27, 1878

We have suffered intolerably from mosquitoes, and yesterday was the climax. It rained steadily all day and we *had* to stay in our tents, and it seemed as if all the mosquitoes in the world might have been summoned to a conference there. The only relief from

---

[1] It was on this trip, according to her account, that Alys (Mrs. Russell), the last of her family to undergo that process, experienced conversion. I should add that she did not attain this condition along the ways pointed out by her parents, but through the efforts of her own will.

them was smoke, and there *are* limits to one's endurance of smoke. So we just had to alternate between mosquitoes and smoke, bearing each one as long as we could, until we had pushed pleasure *far* beyond the verge of pain. And so we determined on a move. For it was forlorn enough to eat at a birch bark table in a dripping rain, even if the table did stand on the bank of a beautiful lake with lovely mountains all around.

Carey and Tom [1] had tramped up 7 miles in a pouring rain, and had stayed all night at a trapper's shanty. And the wind howled, and the trees crashed, and bears dashed past, and their fire would not burn, and it was bitter cold, and the desolation and wildness altogether was enough to have satisfied the most earnest seeker after adventure. Camping out is grand for young people, but *I* am too old !

Such a scatteration as there was of our family circle to make room for this invasion (of 7 unexpected visitors to supper !). We had to gulp down or throw away the remnants of our own suppers, and wash our plates and cups and spoons for our guests. We had some canned salmon served in a tin wash-basin and flap-jacks in a frying-pan, and drawn butter in an empty tomato can, and molasses in an empty yeast powder box, and butter in a tin pail, and salt in a glass jar, and one cup of chocolate for 3 or 4 to drink out of and 1 spoon to several.

August 6, 1878

It is rainy, as usual, and if it were not for this deserted house, we should be utterly uncomfortable. And as to regular camping out, it is a snare and a delusion for anybody over the age of foolishness. I

---

[1] A nephew and niece.

feel myself competent to give advice to all enquirers on the subject of the Adirondacks, and after hearing my advice, they will most likely *stay at home*. I really cannot " 'mire what is not 'mirable ", and I see nothing " 'mirable " in this kind of life for old people. Robert pretends he enjoys it, but as he does absolutely nothing but sit on the piazza and read all day long, I cannot see that it is necessary to come so far to do that. I shall welcome the day of our escape from here with unmitigated joy.

August 10, 1878

We had got about half way up the lake when, in spite of the promising morning, down came the rain as usual, except that if ever the water was poured out of the sky in bucketfuls it was then. Such *sheets* of rain I had never seen before. But since the rain defied us so continually, we determined to defy the rain, and went straight on regardless, wrapping ourselves up in our gum blankets, and ignoring the existence of our feet, which of course were standing in water up to our ankles.

Finally we reached Blue Mountain which is about 2000 feet above the lake, and the view from the top, they say, is very beautiful. *Let it be !* We took our dinner at a little house on Raquette Lake, and then started out to find a shanty for the night, and the rain started with us. It came down in torrents literally. We landed on a lonely shore, and found the shanty we were aiming for already occupied ! And of course the occupants were not going to turn out in that relentless storm for us. We took to our boats again amidst a drenching rain, and rowed across the lake to another point, where we found a shanty, to be sure, but filled with the clothes, guns, cookery utensils and stores of its absent owners.

Necessity knows no law, and we landed and took possession for that one night, trusting the owners would not return. Shelter we *had* to have, by fair means or foul, for the rain came down faster and harder every minute, if that were possible. So we settled ourselves in, the guides made a roaring big fire, and we covered ourselves with our blankets and retired for the night, six of us stretched out in a row on the floor of the shanty, with our feet to the fire.

The young people all managed to sleep, but I could not, and I doubt if I forgot myself for more than half an hour. It was a most *awful* night! Such thunder and lightning I never dreamed could be! It was absolutely continuous from one o'clock until morning, and the wind howled and the water dashed, and it seemed as if the elements were let loose. It was the longest night I ever spent, and I thought if once I should ever get into my own bed in the 3rd storey front of 1315 Filbert Street, I would be about the most thankful woman in the world.

The morning dawned stormier than ever, and we started out in a rain that literally seemed to come down in *sheets*, with one constant roar of the most terrific thunder, and lightning so near that Logan actually saw a tree struck and shivered close beside us on the banks of the lake. . . . Why anybody, having once gone through such experiences should ever want to repeat them, is past *my* finding out. We passed several forlorn looking camps on our way with their forlorn looking occupants sitting in the fronts of their shanties, sad, and desolate, and lonely. I am certain there were many disgusted souls among them, whether they ever confess it or not. . . .

We passed that lady and gentleman that our guide David had left us for, and a more forlorn looking couple I never laid eyes on, to be taking their summer outing. They were sitting side by side in a birch-bark shanty with the smoke of their fire in their eyes, looking out on an awfully lonely lake in the midst of a dismal rain. I could not help exchanging a few words of disgusted sympathy with the poor deluded wife, who responded warmly, and assured me *she did not mean to stay* ! So they have gone in disgust, and David has come back to us.

To Mrs. Henry Ford Barclay

Aet. 46.

THE ADIRONDACKS, *Aug.* 11, 1878

There are hundreds of miles in these mountains as yet untrodden by the foot of man, and many mountain peaks that have never been scaled, unless by the native trapper. I can give you no idea of the utter wildness, the seclusion, and beauty of the whole region. It contains many thousands of square miles of almost unbroken forest . . . Ray has just written a most entertaining letter about our experiences, to a little cousin and I must copy out a page for Girlie.[1] She says describing a walk over one of the " carrys ", " It was perfectly *awful*, and very steep part of the way, and awfully wet.

" There were several little streams that had logs over them, but the streams were so swollen that the logs

---

[1] Daughter of Richard Barclay of Monkhams. She married the Hon. Sir Lancelot Carnegie, son of the 9th Earl of Southesk. After a diplomatic career at Madrid, St. Petersburg, Berlin, Vienna and Paris, he was appointed, in 1924, British Ambassador to Portugal.
L.P.S.

were floating and slipped and rolled under your feet. The water was ankle deep most of the way, and I marched right through it, all heedless of getting my feet soaked through and through. I went ahead of the rest and followed the trail all alone for a long time and thought I was nearly at the end. But at last I sat down on a log to rest and wait. I waited and waited and nobody came, until at last I got scared, and told myself stories of bears coming and eating me up, and how the rest found my skeleton and wept over it, and then it was put in a coffin and lowered down into the earth, and then I was forgotten almost entirely and so on. Well with these grave thoughts I got so frightened that I fairly rushed back a real long way until I met Tom and one of the guides."

(LATER)

We started for Whiteface Mountain about 8.30 in 2 one-horse wagons, and went about 2 miles, over the roughest roads imaginable, part way up the mountain. Then we left our wagons behind and began the climb in real earnest, Mary and I each straddle-legged on our horses. It is impossible to ride on side-saddles up this mountain, the trail is *simply awful*. Thee would not believe it possible for a human being to stick on a horse's back, nor in fact for a horse alone even to get over such a road. It was like going up stairs, all slippery with mud and water, with every now and then a hole broken through into which the horse would plunge almost up to his stomach. It was simply *awful* —no other word will do. But I stuck on, determined not to be daunted, as I knew I could not walk. Once the horse brushed me off under a tree that leaned over the road, but I was not hurt, and mounted again, and stuck on all the tighter.

To Sarah Little

Aet. 47.

PHILADELPHIA, *March* 20, 1879

We are busier than ever, for Logan has added another dog to his collection, a *monstrous* St. Bernard dog this time, who is a perfect houseful, and who demands constant attention. Poor Logan is wellnigh overwhelmed, and we have some funny scenes. All last evening this great creature compelled me to sit and pet him, and every time I tried to do anything else he would put up his huge paw to shake hands, and sweep out of the way all before it, so that I could neither read write nor cipher for a long time. It was a trial.

Mrs. B. is a very interesting woman, but oh ! such a lifetime of doubt as she has had to tell me of ! It was dreadful. I dealt with her doubts in a most summary manner, and actually forced her to give them up like a drunkard his drink.

Sister Sarah, ought thee not to do something for other people, instead of going to so many meetings for thy own enjoyment ?

To Mrs. Lawrence

Aet. 48.

GERMANTOWN, *March* 1880

I fell down 17 steep steps in the middle of the night, head foremost all in the pitch dark ; and on my way down discovered how to fall with the least risk, i.e. let oneself go like a drunken man. I put it in practice, and escaped with only some severe bruises on my forehead and one knee. I *look* like a fright, but *feel* well enough.

To Mrs. Henry Ford Barclay

Aet. 48.

PHILADELPHIA, *March* 10, 1880

The latter part of January Logan and Alys came home for their holidays, bringing with them some of their school friends, and for two weeks we had a merry joyous household. Then my dear mother died rather suddenly after a few days' illness, very quietly and peacefully. And on the day of her funeral Ray [aged 11] was taken with scarlet fever. I think from the first she was stricken with death. Her brain was altogether too active for her little body, and at once the disease went there, not to make her delirious, but to rapidly burn up all her vitality. She was as bright and sweet during the three days of her sickness as ever, and even the last afternoon seemed to possess all her mental powers in perfect vigour. Then suddenly as I was lying beside her singing a hymn, she became unconscious, and passed away most peacefully without a struggle. After death her face was *radiant* with a surprised happy smile, as though she might, just in the moment of going, have caught a glimpse of the dawning glory. I feel a strong conviction that she suddenly saw her grandma who had so lately gone before her ; and I felt at once that she was *at home* ! For myself all was peace. The first moment I knew she was ill I began at once to say " Thy will be done ", " Thy will be done " over and over, and it seemed as if the sweet will of God came down like an enveloping fortress, and hid my soul in an impregnable calm. I know God's choice for my darling is a perfect choice ; and I *know* she had gained by a short and easy road the Home of blessedness towards which the rest of us are travelling with slow and weary steps. And in the face of this knowledge, how can I grieve ? I never did care very much how *I* fared myself, if only my children were happy ; and why should I care now, when a lot so much more blessed than anything my tenderest love could have compassed, has been bestowed upon my darling by the free grace of her God ? On Jan. 9th she wrote (in her Diary) " I am a little bit afraid of the dark (and) I am going to try to overcome it. If I just say to Jesus, when I am in such a position as to frighten me, ' Oh please take care of me, and don't let me be afraid,' and then say the text, ' Let not your heart be troubled, neither let it be afraid,' why then generally I can walk into the darkest corners with only a little bit of trembling. . . . Ah ! who can tell how hard it is to climb the steps where Fame's proud temple shines afar ! Who can ? I wish *I* could, because if it is easy enough I'd like to try.

" A friend of mother's was here to dinner the other day, and they were all talking about woman's voting, and papa said that he thought it would come suddenly. Some woman would rise up above everybody, and put a woman, perhaps herself, into the presidential chair. Oh ! wouldn't *I* like to be that woman ! To have such BURNING eloquence that I would hold my audience in breathless attention, and make everybody think as I think ! That would be the height of my ambition ! I want to make a stir in the world. I'm not content with sitting still, and folding my hands, or being a good little busybody, just being respected and admired in one little corner of the world. And what's more, I *won't* do it if I can *possibly* help it. I know I ought to be content to be famous only to my Lord, but I'm not." . . . Alys [aged 13] wrote a few days afterward, " At first I could *not* say ' Thy will be done ', but I think I can now."

To Mrs. Henry Ford Barclay

Aet. 48.

PORTLAND, OREGON, *July* 23, 1880

We branched off for a day to Salt Lake City, Utah, and had an opportunity of seeing somewhat into the peculiar institutions there. I made a private call on one of Brigham Young's widows, and had a deeply interesting conversation with her. She told me [she] " had been sealed for Eternity to Joseph Smith, and, after his death, had been sealed for time to Brigham Young ". And she seemed to think it was a wonderful advantage they possessed over us Gentiles that they were thus *sure*, by the sealing process, of having a husband throughout Eternity ! But upon further conversation I found her to be a deeply religious woman, who had been led into Mormonism by the hunger of her soul after communion with God and the knowing of His voice. She said she saw this promised in the Bible, and she saw no Christians she knew realised it, and she determined to find it for herself ; and among Mormons she *had* found it to the perfect satisfaction of her soul. And she assured me with the greatest solemnity that if *I* would only honestly seek to know God's will and to know the voice of His Holy Spirit, speaking in my heart, I would be led into Mormonism too !

I could not but be impressed with the woman's evident sincerity, and her loyalty to what she believed to be the truth of God, and I felt that I could never again condemn these people as utter reprobates. Their delusion has taken a very unfortunate form, but it is an honest delusion for all that, and must be dealt with as charitably as we would wish our own especial delusions to be.

To Miss Sarah Beck
Aet. 48.

ESTES PARK, COLORADO, *Aug.* 18, 1880

I have had a great deal to do with incompatible people, and I soon found that I should be in condemnation all the while unless the Lord taught me the art of associating with them harmoniously. And true to His promise to make a way in every temptation, He taught me this lesson—to *settle down* to the peculiarities of people as I would to heaviness of lead, and to be no more provoked at the manifestation of these peculiarities, than I would be at the manifestation of the weight of lead.

Since then as soon as I find anything disagreeable in the make-up of people, I accept it as part of them, and do not *expect* anything else ; and commit it to the Lord, asking Him to make the trial and discipline it brings just the medicine I need at that time. In this way incompatible people have become my chief means of grace, and many a time I have turned them into chariots, or rather the Lord has, which have carried me to places of triumph over self that I could have reached in no other way.

To her sister, Sarah Nicholson
Aet. 48.

Sept. 18, 1880

I have had a revelation about guidance that seems to make obedience a far simpler thing. It has come to me through seeing the fatally sad mistakes made by so many. It is this—that the voice of God comes through our *judgment*, and not through our *impressions*. Our impressions may coincide with our judgments or they may not, but it is through the latter *alone* that God's voice comes. And when people go by impressions in opposition to their judgments, they are turning from the true voice of God, to follow the false voices of self, or of evil spirits, or of morbid conscience, or of some evil influence from other people. It *is* said in the Bible that He will guide the meek in judgment, and it is not said that He will guide them in impressions or feelings.

I believe this going by impressions always leads either into fanaticism as with S. F. S.[1] and others, or into insanity as with the Friends. While the people who are led by God through their judgments make very few mistakes. Think of this and tell me thy views. Now in the matter of novels thee and I only have impressions to go by. Our judgment tells us that a moderate reading of novels is a good thing as preserving the mind from overwork in one direction. And as a *fact*, my best work both in preaching and writing has been done while I was taking the occasional recreation of reading good novels. When I was writing " Frank " I kept a novel [2] by me to read in whenever I grew tired of writing.

To her sister, Sarah Nicholson
Aet. 49.

GERMANTOWN, *Mar.* 3, 1881

But, Sally, you *cannot* love if you *do not*. You can so bring the Lord in as to lose all sight of the person,

---

[1] She is probably alluding to what, in her posthumous book, *Religious Fanaticism*, she refers to as " Miss S's Fanaticism "—in fact to the old lady mentioned in the note on p. 6.

[2] This statement is more startling than it might be thought. " All fiction of every kind," she wrote (*The Unselfishness of God*, p. 128), " was considered by the Friends of those days to be ' pernicious ', and on this point our mother was very strict, and we were not allowed to read even the most innocent and select Sunday-school stories. As to novels, the very word was felt to be wicked, and to this day I never use it without a momentarily instinctive feeling of lawlessness, as if I were deliberately doing something wrong."

and can be perfectly sweet and compassionate towards the person, but as to loving or respecting that which does not win love and respect and does not deserve it, you just *cannot*, and that is the long and short of it. For instance, A. C., suppose it was my lot to live with her and bear things from her, or M. O., I could so see the Lord in it all as to be perfectly victorious, and also to be tenderly compassionate towards them, but I COULD NOT love nor respect them.

To Miss Priscilla Mounsey

Aet. 49.

ROCKY MOUNTAINS, *July* 18, 1881

We are quite a large party and are travelling with quite an array; first go 4 horseback riders, then a large mountain wagon with 6 of us in it, then 3 baggage wagons with our tents, beds, provisions, stove, etc., etc., and finally a dog to guard our camps named " Buster ". We have 4 Guides and a cook, and are 9 ourselves, so we form quite a cavalcade.

The great excitement of our day is to find a good place to camp for the night where we shall have wood for a camp fire, water to drink, and grass for our 12 horses. When we settle on a place we all have to go to work. The men unloose the horses, and unload the wagons, and put up the tents; the cook gets out his stove and begins preparations for supper; the boys pick up their guns and rifles and go off to hunt something for us to eat; the girls pick up wood for the fire, and I make the beds of blankets and buffalo robes, and get out the night wrappings. We are travelling in an utterly wild country with antelopes, and deer, and elk, and even bears all around us, though the latter do not come very near our camp. But the excitement of finding our way and of getting across the streams and over the mountains, and the adventures of the boys out hunting, make up pretty full days.

To her sister, Sarah Nicholson

Aet. 49.

YELLOWSTONE PARK, *Aug.* 13, 1881

I am awfully sorry M. has missed all this, and yet I am *sure* she could not have stood it. It is simple misery to me, and I have had a wretched time with my digestion. I really would have gone to bed if I had been at home, but I just had to keep on and stand it. I prayed for wisdom to know what to do and at last bethought me of some pills as a tonic which Dr. D. had put up for me, and they have acted like a charm, so that now I am pretty well. But how long it will last there is no telling. We have had some rainy weather and just had to ride and eat and sleep in a perfect soak. Why we are not all *ill* I cannot tell, but it was the concentrated essence of discomfort, *that* I know. . . .

As to there being no fruition in life, I am not worried about *that*, for I do not think this life is meant for fruition. . . . Look at Mother, for instance, she just lived the ordinary round, kept house, brought up her children, was kind to her friends, but this was all ; she did no especial work, and made no mark anywhere ; but I have no doubt she fulfilled her mission in this nursery stage, and it would have been folly for her to have bewailed herself.

I feel as if I had carried this camping-out party through by prayer. So many perils have beset us on every hand that I do not know what I could have done if I could not have prayed. So I have concluded I *do* pray about almost everything, though I had never especially noticed it. But *united* prayer with other people I confess I do not care for, and I have told Mrs. Little so and she doesn't expect it of me. She and Cad [1] keep it up by the hour sometimes, but I tell them their prayers get answered upside down often. They and Sarah Smiley met *every day* one summer to pray that *I* might not become " Broad Church ", and I kept getting broader and broader, and finally they got Broad themselves.

To her friends

Aet. 49.

YELLOWSTONE PARK, *Aug.* 18, 1881

Our cook, Tin Lee, is a great feature of these camp-fire entertainments. Sometimes we get him to sing a Chinese song (he calls it " songing a sing ") and a sadder and more pathetic tune I have never heard anywhere. It is always the same tune, and has no variations, and it seems to embody in its sad refrain all the grief of a hopeless race.

The night air is always cool enough to make the warmth agreeable and the deliciousness of lying stretched out on one's buffalo robes under the open sky, around a bright roaring fire, can only be understood by experience. It seems, too, as if everyone's wits were sharper than usual under such circumstances and our young party have many grand nights that give the three quiet elders almost as much delight as themselves.

The only drawback is the inevitable coming of 10 o'clock, which I always consider the good time for going to bed. The sound of my " Now, daughters, it

[1] Carrie, her cousin, Mrs. Lawrence, one of the " Five Mystic Birds " (see note on p. 81).

is bedtime ", is almost as much dreaded as the cry of
a panther would be.   There is only one other sound
that spreads greater consternation, and that is the call
of Tin Lee in the morning when breakfast is ready,
and he wakes us up from our delicious morning naps
by playing a tattoo on a tin pan, and calling out to us
at the top of his funny squeaky voice :   " Hi there !
Breakfast !   Flappee jack !   Flappee jack !   Him all
done ! "

These Rocky Mountain parks are wonderfully beautiful things.   Imagine an English nobleman's country
seat set right down in the midst of mountains, with
great stretches of greenest grass, groups of beautiful
trees, beds of brightest flowers, a winding, dashing
mountain river, tiny lakes, slopes of turf, fantastic rocks
scattered in the most romantic confusion, and around
it all a girdle of grandest mountains, often flecked with
snow and changing continually from sunshine to storm,
one hour covered with clouds, and the next standing
out in clear-cut beauty and sublimity against the deep
blue sky.   The Rocky Mountains will always stand
out in my memory as the emblem of all this world can
give of peace and beauty and perfect rest.

At Tower Creek all possibility of taking the wagon
any further was at an end, and there was no alternative
but to mount one of those wild beasts named by Adam
a horse, and pursue the journey on horseback !   The
guides picked me out a sober old creature named
Foxy, used to carrying a pack, and therefore equal to
my weight, while not likely to be frisky or foolish.

On the morning of the 9th day of August we left
Tower Creek, and started, a long train of 26 horses
with their colts, and 2 dogs, for the Yellowstone Falls
and Cañon.   As I was quite determined never to go
out of a walk, on account of my tendency to slip off,

I took the extreme rear of the pack train, and plodded on very contentedly, finding myself far more comfortable than I could have hoped.

But alas ! my comfort was of but short duration, for when we were about to stop for a lunch at the foot of Mount Washburn, Foxy lost sight of the pack train to which he felt he rightfully belonged, and getting either bewildered or angry, I could not tell which, he began to behave in the most unaccountable and uncomfortable manner. He backed and forwarded, and sidled, and turned round and round, and neighed and completely mastered me, until one of the guides came up and attaching a rope to his bridle led him the rest of the way.

It was a most beautiful ride across the wooded pass over Mount Washburn, and but for Foxy I should have greatly enjoyed it. I believe the rest of the party were enthusiastic in their delight, but from my uncomfortable and precarious seat on Foxy's back everything wore a sombre aspect. Then too it rained or drizzled all the afternoon, and we went into camp at night with grass and trees almost as wet as if it had been a swamp. But in this forest and on that grass we had to make our beds and go to sleep. And strange to say most of us had as comfortable a night as in our own beds at home, though I confess my old bones ached sometimes, and to turn over was an event.

On the 10th we reached the Yellowstone Falls, and camped near the Cañon. To the north it disappears in a sharper turn, and penetrates, they say, grander and wilder scenes, and one can see the mighty walls, rendered gloomy by the distant shadows that overhang its awful depths. But to the south, and all around and beneath, there is no gloom, only " grandeur steeped in beauty ". And at certain hours in the morning, when the sun strikes the foam and spray of the cataract, the whole cañon at its foot is one glorious giant abyss of rainbows, shifting and changing with every breath of wind.

This cañon presents another aspect to a parent's mind, however, which must not be overlooked. There are of course no railings along the dizzy edges of these awful heights and depths, and as young people *will* always go just as near the edge of things as they can, it cannot be said to be comfortable to take a party like ours into such a scene of temptation.

Both Robert and I felt truly thankful for every hour of safety while we remained in this neighbourhood. The young fellows of our party found great delight in starting enormous fallen trees down the awful incline, and watching them crash their way with a fearful swiftness to the river's bank. Any *Mother* will know how that made me feel, specially when I add that no doctor could be procured in that region under 7 days at the very least, and that we had neither houses nor beds, nor any of the things considered necessary in sickness. I could not bear to spoil the enjoyment of the young people by unnecessary fussiness, but I confess I was thankful every minute that our family did not possess a country seat on the banks of the Yellowstone Cañon ! Often, all I could do was just to walk away and sit down with my back to things, and commit the whole company of juniors to the care of their Father in Heaven.

The day we left the Yellowstone Cañon we travelled about 12 or 15 miles to a point on the banks of the Yellowstone River, about 6 miles below the lake, I on the back of Foxy, at the tail end of the pack train. The miseries I endured on the back of that creature would fill a volume. A great deal of this misery arose from the fact that every muscle ached with the unusual position ; and from this of course there was no relief. Then the trails were often so steep, and the gullies we had to cross so deep and abrupt, and the saddle so slippery that it was only by sheer force of character I could keep on at all. Moreover, the moment that knowing animal lost sight of the pack train he would presume on my innocence, and begin a series of the most harrowing manœuvres, that baffled me utterly, and I felt that literally and truly I was at his mercy. Once he gave an unexpected jump, and I went right over his back to the ground under his feet. But providentially he stood still after this feat, and as I have learned *how* to fall by just letting myself go, I escaped with only an unimportant bruise. Yet such was the inexorableness of circumstances, that there was literally nothing left for me to do but to pick myself up and climb on that dreadful back again.

At this Two Ocean Pass camp my miseries from Foxy came to an end. For here the wagon road began again, and as our wagon had been sent around to meet us, I once more found myself (which I confess I had hardly expected) respectably seated behind a pair of steady-going mules, jogging along over a good road. No words can express the relief it was. Neither can any words express strongly enough my unspoken resolve at that place never again under any circumstances to mount the back of any creature, whether called a horse or a lion !

NOTE I (p. 30)

Robert Pearsall Smith, though it was never believed that he had gone to lengths which could be reckoned as sinful, had compromised himself with a female disciple. Of this disaster, Logan Pearsall Smith writes in *Unforgotten Years* : " ' Salute one another with a holy kiss ', Paul enjoined upon the Romans, and it has taken Christianity centuries to eliminate from its proceedings this holy kiss—if indeed it has succeeded in doing so completely. Certainly in my father's time this exquisite secret doctrine was extremely prevalent in America ; and my father, in spite of my mother's almost desperate warnings, would expound it to select gatherings mostly composed of spinsters of a certain age. Unluckily one of these grew jealous of another, and let the great beautiful cat out of the bag, to the scandal of the righteous, and the extreme joy of the unholy, whose jokes about the ' Higher Life ' as it was called, made my father feel that it would be wise for him to cease his ministrations."

But following this blow, Robert Pearsall Smith lost more than his occupation ; he lost his faith as well. His son has told me how, to this disbelieving and disillusioned preacher, believing disciples would still come for guidance : and how, though he beseeched them not to desert him, his children would steal mischievously away, and leave him to the awkward task of giving advice and encouragement of which he himself hardly believed a word.

V

THE AMERICAN SCENE

To Mrs. Anna Shipley

Aet. 50.

GERMANTOWN, *Jan.* 11, 1882

Oh, Anna, my heart just aches for the misery, pure unmitigated misery, there is in this world. Thee sees *I* get below the surface and know. And as I sit in those meetings, and see the " old stagers ", as thee calls them, come in, I know of the awful sorrows that lie hidden in those apparently calm lives, and I could cry for every one of them.

Only the other day I looked at a row of them who happened to be sitting together and every one of them *I* knew, though no one else did, had husbands who made their lives, as far as the earthly side of it goes, one long torture. What is invalidism compared to *that* ? No, beloved, suffering is the universal lot, and we may well be thankful, it is no worse for us individually than it is.

Oscar Wilde is a " sell ". He looks like two radishes set up on their thin ends. He does say now and then a fine thing about art, just about what I would say about religion. But his manner is so poor and his style so excessively " Rose Matilda " that I believe everybody is disgusted. Logan did not get *one* idea from him, but I got several. For instance, he said— " To the true artist there is no time but the artistic moment ; and no land but the land of beauty." There is a meaning in this, but what could *Logan* make out of it ? And such a Logan !

To Miss Priscilla Mounsey

Aet. 50.

GERMANTOWN, *Jan.* 8, 1882

The loneliness thou speaks of I know. For do not think, darling, that it is confined to unmarried people. It is just as real in lives that have plenty of human ties, husbands, and children and friends. It is the loneliness of this *world life*, the loneliness of hearts that are made for union with God, but which have not yet fully realised it. I believe it is inseparable from humanity. I believe God has ordained it in the very nature of things by creating us for Himself alone. And I believe He very rarely allows any human love to be satisfying, just that this loneliness may drive us to Him. I have noticed that when a human love *is* satisfying something always comes in to spoil it. Either there is death, or there is separation, or there is a change of feeling on one side or the other or something, and the heart is driven out of its human resting place on to God alone.

Sometimes God permits a little taste of a satisfying love to a human being, but I do not believe it ever lasts long. I do not mean that the *love* may not last, but separation comes in some way, and the perfect *satisfaction* is taken out of it. Now, darling, thy loneliness is not *only* because thou art unmarried and hast no very close human ties, it is the loneliness of a heart made for God but which has not yet reached its full satisfaction in Him. Human love might *for awhile* satisfy thee, but it would not last.

If thou can only see this and *settle down* to it, it will help thee very much. Thou wilt give up, as I have, any expectation of finding satisfaction in the creature, and will no longer suffer with disappointment at not finding it. And this will deliver thee from the worst part of the *suffering* of loneliness. Thee will accept it as a God-given blessing meant only to drive thee to Himself.

Thy loneliness is only different in *kind* but not in *fact* from the loneliness of every human heart apart from God. Thy circumstances *are* lonely, but thy loneliness of spirit does not come from these, it is the loneliness of humanity. Therefore *nothing* but God can satisfy it. No change of circumstances, no coming in of the dearest earthly ties even, not *my* continued presence even, could really satisfy for any length of time the hungry depths of thy soul. I am speaking, darling, out of the depths of my own experience when I say this, and thee may believe me.

To Miss Priscilla Mounsey
Aet. 50.

GERMANTOWN, *Jan.* 22, 1882

If I were with thee, my precious child, I would make thee give up all future *self-reflective acts*. By this I mean all thinking over either thy successes or thy failures. The moment the action is passed, forget it, and pass on to the next. If thee does not understand just what I mean here, tell me, and I will explain more fully. It is the rule of my life never to think over my past action. This saves me all temptations to self-elation, and all temptations to discouragement, and enables me to live continually in the present moment with God.

In the evening I preached to a great crowded church in the city and had to go all alone. I wanted *thee*, darling! And of course I left my gum shoes in the pulpit, and had to be run after out to the street by somebody to bring them.

To Mrs. Lawrence
Aet. 50.

YOSEMITE VALLEY, *Aug.* 5, 1882

Carrie, do let us cultivate ourselves into being *nice* old people. One secret I am sure is always to take the part of the young, and I intend to do this more and more. Right or wrong, they shall have my *sympathy*, and help in the former. I wonder if thee could not come to an understanding with thy mother. I had to with mine. I just told her plain out that she must not interfere in my children's lives and I advised her not to criticise my management of them. I told her it would not change my management in the least, and it would only make unpleasant feelings. She cried, and it was very hard for me and for her too, but it worked like a charm and was far happier for her as well as the rest of us ever afterwards. That continual interfering ruins a household, and it gets worse as people grow older. I think Mother really loved me better after that than before. She laid down the *responsibility* of things, and it was a relief to her.

Is it not strange, Carrie, that in this world we cannot do really kind and Christlike things without getting into trouble? We may do a thing in a business way and it turns out a great success; but do the same thing as a kindness, and it is sure to make a muss somehow. I would love to open my house to all the distressed saints if I could, but if I did, it would just end in trouble, I suppose.

To Mrs. Henry Ford Barclay
Aet. 50.

GERMANTOWN, *Oct.* 18, 1882

I do not think myself it is any harm to be proud of our children, when our pride takes the form of thankfulness to our Heavenly Father for His goodness in giving us such lovely gifts. But I may tell thee confidentially that I do not expect any of my children to live many years. Whether this is because I have lost so many that I feel it natural they should die, or whether it is prophecy I do not know. It does not worry me at all, but I confess it *does* make me indulgent.

The other day when I was fixing up Mary's room at College, she wanted me to buy her a leather covered arm chair. I did not think she needed it, and was going to refuse, when she coughed. Immediately I thought " Now perhaps she will die of consumption, and then how I shall wish I had bought her the chair." So forthwith I bought it. And when it came home I said, " There, daughter, thee coughed up that chair." I tell thee this that thee may know just what a foolish mother I am. I tell the children that Heavenly Father will have to give them their discipline, for their earthly parents have not the heart to do it.

To Miss Priscilla Mounsey

Aet. 51.

Jan. 10, 1883

Oh, darling, do pray that I may never be so far " left to myself " as to start a newspaper. I am actually afraid that sometime I will, everybody seems so driven to it !

Lady Mount Temple is about as sweet as a human being can be. But she is a spiritualist, and told me that nothing had saved her from absolute infidelity but the proofs she had seen in spiritualism of a life in another region. I undertook to " labour " with her once, but she turned round and " laboured " with me, and had so much Scripture on her side, that I concluded prudence was the better part of valour, and said nothing more.

Journal Letter to her friends

Aet. 51.

MAINE, *Aug.* 8, 1883

I will write a Journal Letter for the information, edification, commiseration and admiration of my sisters and friends, and it may go the rounds. Our yacht is a tiny steamer with a little cabin large enough for our party of 10 to crowd into for our meals, and for the 7 females to sleep on the floor at night. But our first night out we decided to sleep on shore and viewed the putting up of our tent and the piling up of our fresh hemlock beds with complacency, and quite looked forward to the night. But alas ! we left the mosquitoes and " minges " as the Guides call them, altogether out of our calculations, and it was a night of cruel disappointments. *Simple misery* would best express our condition of mind and body.

We preferred the cabin floor thereafter to the softest bed of hemlock boughs that could be dreamed of. For by pushing the yacht out away from the shore we escape all the insects of every kind. Imagine a little cabin about 12 by 8 [feet] as the sleeping place of *seven* good sized " female women ", 2 on tiny lounges and 5 on the floor, and you will know there could not be much spare room nor spare comfort. But it is all fun to the children, and *I* grin and bear it.

One day we made a trip to a Logging Camp on the Nahhoodus river. To get there, we had to walk 4 miles through the primeval forest over a rough logging road. And I want you to imagine me pegging doggedly along, with a dark blue felt hat on my head, a staff in my hand, and groans in my heart, which I valiantly repressed lest I should spoil the fun of the rest. The groans I have thus repressed at various times during this trip would have furnished David Updegraff (that excitable Quaker preacher) with enough for several series of his revival meetings, I verily think.

I honestly *do* believe that this time *is* the last time I shall take a camping-out trip. For I find my stiff knees and other accessories of old age make it too tiresome for even me to enjoy. But I suppose you will not believe me ; and in fact, I hardly believe myself. When summer comes, and the children get after me, I seem to lose all my backbone, and yield myself up an easy martyr. We have had grand camp fires at our camp, and they *are* delightful, at least to all youthful minds. They were attended with some drawbacks to *me*, I must confess. In the first place, I had no comfortable place to sit, as logs without any backs to them, or stones are not the most luxurious of seats to matrons over 50 years of age. And then the clash-ma-clabbers were not always of the most " filling " nature to a mature mind, and I had therefore nothing to do but to hold Quaker meeting between times, and wonder how soon I might dare to propose bed to the youthful party.

Towards the end of our trip we met Professor Phelps and his party, which consisted of Professor Farnham of Yale, and the Rev. Newman Smyth, the author of " Old Faiths in a New Light ", a *grand* book on Christian evolution.

I think I told you a few months ago that I wrote to Newman Smyth asking him to explain, if he could, why God forbade Adam and Eve from coming to the knowledge of good and evil. I said in my letter that it seemed to me a necessary step in development, and that I should have thought God would have *wanted* them to come to it ; that they would have been mere animals otherwise. He had never answered this letter so when I met him, I introduced myself and asked him if he had received it. He said " Yes ", and that he had it in his trunk at Mount Kineo, meaning to answer it this summer, if he could see clearly what to say, but that as yet he did not. He said he was thinking about it and felt sure he would have something to say concerning it soon. He said no one had ever spoken to him on the subject before, though he had often wondered that they had not. He promised to write me as soon as he had any light, and asked me to do the same.

He is a delightful man, and my short conversation with him interested me exceedingly. But, oh, girls, *what* a guy I looked like. It is painful to think of. *They* were just going into the woods in all the neatness and cleanliness of new outfits, and *we* were just coming out, in rags and dirt, draggled and blowsy and forlorn. For once, I *did* care for looks ; and I really feel as if the man would conclude I was not worth writing to after all, even if he should get an idea on the subject. Clothes *do* make a difference, there is no denying it.

To her family

Aet. 51.

MARTHA'S VINEYARD, MASS., *Aug.* 30, 1883

This is a place about like Ocean Grove, but the meetings must be much smaller, for the one last night was a very meagre affair. The sermon was a *denunciatory* one that was calculated in my opinion to drive sinners away from the God depicted in it ; and apparently it did, for with all their coaxing they could not get a single person old or young up to the altar. The preacher asked all who loved Christ to hold up their hands and keep them up, and then he sent people down through the audience to speak to those who had not raised a hand and invite them forward. But it was all of no avail, forward they would not go. Then he drew a blood-curdling picture of the awfulness of *thus* rejecting God's offers of mercy.

He certainly tried the " terror " plan, which David Updegraff says is the *only* effectual way, most fully and vigorously. It fairly made me heartsick, and I wondered how God could endure it to be so misrepresented, but the text came to my mind " the times of this ignorance God winked at " and it comforted me. Especially as I knew He had nothing much but ignorance to wink at in all of us all our lives long.

After the sermon, I was introduced to the preacher and determined to " upset his theology " by asking him my question. So I said that I had noticed he had said in the course of his sermon that the thing which distinguishes a man from a beast is his free moral agency, and I asked him if this free moral agency did not necessitate a knowledge of good and evil ? " Most certainly it does," was his reply, " and that is just where man shows his divine origin," etc., etc. Then I said, " Why did God forbid man to come to that knowledge ? And why is it called a ' fall ' when he did come to it ? Did not God Himself say after it was done ' Man has now become *as one of us* to know good and evil ? ' " For once the preacher was nonplussed, but rallying himself he said, " Oh, that only meant actually doing evil, it meant the experimental knowledge that comes from doing it. Of course man knew about good and evil before that." " Then," I said,

" was that experimental knowledge the kind God had, for He said man had come to *His* kind of knowledge." " Yes," he replied, " it was." " What," I said, " had God actually *done* the wrong thing ? " " Oh, no, I did not mean that," he answered. And then I took pity on him and said, " Well, thanks, that is something to think about. Good night," and walked off. He called out after me, " I never thought of the subject before so have only answered your questions off hand." " Well," I called back, " think of it now and see what will come to you about it."

To her sister, Sarah Nicholson

Aet. 53.

GERMANTOWN, *Mar.* 12, 1885

Thy letter dictated to Madge [1] fell like a knell upon my heart. And I immediately made up my mind that I would let thee die if thee could, and would not be so hatefully selfish as to try to keep thee in thy poor suffering body one day longer. But what I shall do without thee I cannot tell ; for I assure thee, life looks like a dreary pilgrimage if I am to walk through the rest of it without my twin.

Poor Charles Coffin was here last night, and, oh Sarah, what trouble he has had and is having. Then Rendel Harris was here too and he has just sent in his resignation, and it is probable that he and Helen will have to take up their march again, and find a new home and new work. Then there was Robert—three *doctrinaire* men, all three quite eminent in the religious world, and all three under a cloud. It did seem rather odd. I told them the trouble with them was

---

[1] Madge Nicholson, her niece.

that they had all been righteous overmuch ; they had not mixed in enough of the world in their religion. Thee and I have had such a spice of the old Adam in all our religion that we have never been able to quite turn the corner into the region of extra piety. I am sure that has been my salvation many a time. We were made to be human beings here, and when people try to be anything else, they generally get into some sort of scrapes.

To her sister, Sarah Nicholson

Aet. 53.

GERMANTOWN, *Mar.* 15, 1885

I fairly ache for one of our good old-fashioned pow-wows, when we have so often settled our own affairs and everybody else's, with the words at the end of all our talk, " Well, I'm sure I don't know."

To her sister, Sarah Nicholson

Aet. 53.

GERMANTOWN, *Mar.* 28, 1885

Sarah, I want to ask thee a solemn question. Did thee ever one single time have thy Bank book balance and thy own cheque book balance agree exactly ? Do not tell, but *I* never did.

To her friends

Aet. 54.

LONDON, *Feb.* 7, 1886

Busy, busy, busy is the word that best describes my life in London. Busy with house fixing, busy with people, busy with meetings, busy with a thousand

G

interests of every kind. Too busy in this busy London to get one tenth part of the things done that I want to do.

While I was at Broadlands a young niece of Lady Mount Temple's came in who is a London belle just now, and is in the midst of the gayest life possible. I was very much interested in talking with her, and trying to get at the true inwardness of her life. She had been at a Ball a few nights before and danced with Prince Edward and Prince George, the sons of the Prince of Wales, several times. She said they were "very nice young fellows".

She is named Agnita, and is living with her sister Lady Hastings, her chaperone to all her dissipations. I asked her how often she saw her chaperone during the evenings, and she said only when they arrived at a place and when they left, and that having chaperones was a perfect farce. I asked how many Ball dresses she had to have for the "Season", and she said about six would do by freshening them up every time. She said she did not dare to dance with any man more than twice, or remarks would be made, and the men, she said, were always afraid of being entrapped by the girls, and so avoided them. This was what I had always heard, but could not believe ; but I suppose it must be true if such a girl as this says so.

Agnita said she often danced all night, from 11 until 5, and this, night after night, and she never felt tired and never was bored either. I looked with amazement upon a human being who could give such a record of her life and think it all right. And yet she seemed like a nice girl, too. Well, lives *are* different !

VI

THE GAY WORLD

To her friends

Aet. 54.

LONDON, *Feb.* 14, 1886

Last Monday the " Unemployed " workmen of London had a Demonstration at Trafalgar Square, and I attended it. There were lots of young men from 18 to 21 who were up to all sorts of tricks, and when the meeting broke up these rowdies somehow stole a march on the Police and rioted through one or two of the West End streets, breaking windows and " looting " the shops.

No one thinks it was bonâ fide working-men at all who did this rioting, but only the rowdies who always hang on the skirts of a crowd. But it frightened London out of all its senses for a day or two. I never saw such a frightened set of people. I went shopping the next day and had it all to myself pretty much. The shops were all barricaded, and nobody was out shopping but me, and London seemed paralysed. And there was not the slightest sign of any rioting anywhere. It was as striking a case of shutting the stable door after the horse was stolen as I ever saw.

To her friends

Aet. 54.

LONDON, *Feb.* 19, 1886

On Tuesday Mary and I went to a Hunt : I have always wanted to see an English Hunt that I might know how to picture it when I should read about it ; and when I saw in the Monday papers that the Queen's staghounds would hunt a stag from a place called Redhill not very far from London, I determined to go, and Mary concluded to go with me. A good many horses went down on the train with us, also their owners, both ladies and gentlemen. Mary and I sat in the same carriage with a young lady all attired for the Hunt in waistcoat, cravat and round top hat, with her riding dress on and her whip in her hand. There were 2 or 3 gentlemen with her, and we soon found from their conversation that she was a sister of Lord Randolph Churchill. It was just the morning after Lord Randolph had made what is considered by the Liberals a most revolutionary speech, in Belfast, and it was very interesting to hear his sister and her friends discussing " Randolph " and his plans for the Irish.

One of the men appeared to be the owner of one of the houses that had suffered during the riots, and he said the ignominy of it was almost worse than the damage ; that he would not have minded half so much if his windows had been broken by genuine stones, but to have legs of mutton and loaves of bread dashed through one's drawing room windows was a little too much.

When we arrived at Uxbridge station we took a cab and drove 2 miles to Redhill, in the midst of a lovely rolling country with lovely English lanes winding off in every direction. Gentlemen and ladies were gathering to the Meet from all sides, and a great wagon full of the Hounds was awaiting the arrival of the poor stag. This was brought in a cart from the herds in Windsor Park, I believe, and was turned loose in a ploughed field. Men and boys gathered around to frighten it and to set it off on a run, and as soon as this was fairly accomplished, the hounds were let loose and the Hunt began. The poor frightened stag ran this way and that, and the dogs and horses followed, riding over fields and jumping hedges and ditches perfectly regardless of where they went, only so that they followed the hounds. M. and I followed on foot, as well and as far as we could, and really felt a little of the hunting spirit. But of course the hunt soon outstripped us, and we got into our cab and drove back to the station, having seen all we wanted.

I shall always understand about hunts now and I can easily see how excited the English people get over them. But there must be a great many accidents, with such reckless riding and jumping. Juliet says the deer are never killed, only run down until they are tired, and she thinks they rather like the fun. But I cannot help feeling it is a cruel sport.

To her friends

Aet. 54.

BERLIN, *March* 7, 1886

I went with Logan last evening to a concert. The music was very fine, Logan said, and it did sound nice, but my inward ear for music has never been opened yet, and I confess I did not particularly enjoy it. Logan says that is an evolution I shall have to get in Heaven. And I suppose I must, if I am to enjoy the harps there. At present, I confess, a very short exercise in harp playing suffices me.

Yesterday morning Logan took me to the picture gallery [1] here, and I saw Rembrandts and Titians and

---

[1] " I certainly grew up believing that it was wicked to go to picture galleries, or to look at a statue. And I remember well, when I was about seventeen, breaking loose from all the traditions of my life and

Tintorets and Claud Lorraines, etc. etc. And I may as well tell the truth at once and say that *I do not like them* ! I am sure if any modern painter were to paint such poor pictures now, he would be hooted out of the profession. I forgot to say that in Antwerp I saw several of Reubens' pictures, and they simply disgusted me. They were great fat masses of coarse flesh. The babies were like pigs for coarseness, and in one or two of his Christs, the anatomy was repulsive. I think of course the " Old Masters " were wonderful considering how long ago they painted, etc. etc. ; but that is not the orthodox style of praise, I know, so I do not hope to build any reputation on it.

To her friends

Aet. 54.

DRESDEN, *Mar.* 10, 1886

Logan and Harry Thomas [1] and I all three went to the picture gallery together, and I saw the Sistine Madonna of Raphael. I am thankful to say that I liked it. I confess I was awfully afraid I should not,

going with a beating heart, as though on some perilously wicked excursion, into the Academy of Fine Arts in Philadelphia. There was a marble group there of Hero and Leander, and I am afraid Leander had not many clothes on, and I can see myself now, standing and looking at it with my heart in my mouth, and saying to myself ' I suppose now I shall go straight to hell, but I cannot help it. If I must go there, I must, but I *will* look at this statue.' No words can express what a daring sinner I felt myself to be ; and I remember distinctly that I was quite surprised to find myself outside that Academy, standing unharmed in Broad Street, without having experienced the swift judgments of an offended Creator." (*Unselfishness of God*, p. 133.)
L.P.S.

[1] Son of H.W.S.'s sister Mary, who had married Dr. James Carey Thomas, of Baltimore, and was the mother of Martha Carey Thomas, the most famous of all the famous Whitall women. [She became Dean and President of Bryn Mawr College.] L.P.S.

and I had determined not to pretend to if I did not, so that I feared I should have to encounter the scorn of my two youthful cavaliers. Logan is a staunch adherent of the Old Masters, but Harry comforted me up by telling me that his mother had felt about as I do, and had marched through the galleries of the Old Masters with her skirts drawn closely around her in a fine contempt.

I really would like to know what *is* the bottom truth about all this fuss that is made over the Old Masters. Is it just a fashion, such as makes even ugly ways of dressing look beautiful when once we have been convinced it is " the thing " ? Or is it a real fact that any painting which looks so inferior, can really be, in some occult way, so infinitely superior ? I confess I cannot help believing in the first hypothesis. But Logan says I am like a child who thinks Mother Goose's rhymes far superior poetry to Shakespeare ; and of course this is possible, for I know I have no education in art. But still—when the thing is right there before my eyes how *can* I believe I am so deceived ?

To her friends

Aet. 54.

PRAGUE, *Mar.* 15, 1886

The streets in Prague are narrow, and they wind around the houses and through them in dark vaulted passages, that continually suggest mysteries and dungeons and ambushes, and all sorts of foreign things. It is as great a contrast as could be to dear old straight-angled, broad-streeted, frank-faced Philadelphia, where it is hard to believe anything mysterious could possibly happen . . . I was more interested in the old Jewish

Cemetery than anything else. It is 1300 years old and looks as if it had been untouched all that time. It is right in the midst of the town, and the effect of such a weird and silent wilderness in the heart of a noisy city was indescribable. I confess I love grave-yards, that are such an unanswerable proof that we *shall* get rid of these old cocoons sometime. The sight of them always gives me a thrill of delight, and I almost felt as if I should like to move into this one and live there.

To her friends

Aet. 54.

VIENNA, *Mar.* 17, 1886

I would never travel here for pleasure again. Either give me home with all its comforts, or a foreign country that looks and seems really foreign. I have not even had the satisfaction of boiling over with indignation at seeing a woman and a cow hitched together pulling a cart with a man walking alongside driving them, which I have always heard was a feature of these countries. The women, however, do seem to do more outdoor work than with us. I have seen them stirring mortar for buildings, and even carrying it up ladders in hods. But then the men did it too, so that I could not boil over at that.

To Mrs. Lawrence

Aet. 54.

VIENNA, *Mar.* 18, 1886

I am rejoiced at my sister Sarah's escape from her poor sick cocoon, and I do not allow myself to grieve for one instant. It is such a comfort to me to know that she is having a good time, for I have sympathised so intensely with all her long years of trial and suffering that I never could enjoy anything thoroughly for thinking of her deprivations. She has never had her fair share of Mary's and my fun. But now she has got ahead of us at last and is having an infinitely better time than we are, and how could I be anything but glad ?

Our five mystic birds [1] can never meet on this earth again and talk of our flights. One has gone on a flight indeed, from which there is no returning to tell the tale. But it does make the world feel lonely, does it not, to have her out of it ? Oh, if I could only go too ! I cannot tell thee how I long to go. The thought of living to old age is perfectly appalling to me, and I have to say " Thy will be done " hard whenever I think of it.

To her daughter, Mary Costelloe (Berenson)

Aet. 54.

CONSTANTINOPLE, *Mar.* 30, 1886

I have just got back (from a call). I went in a Sedan chair lined with yellow silk and felt like a Harem woman.

To her friends

Aet. 54.

ISLAND OF CORFU, *Apr.* 13, 1886

We took a boat (to a most picturesque little island with an old monastery on its highest point) and were charmed with its lovely beauty. We found living

[1] H.W.S. herself, her sisters Sarah Nicholson and Mary Thomas, and Mrs. Little, and her cousin, Mrs. Lawrence. L.P.S.

there one old Monk, the only survivor of the Brother-hood, who leads a hermit life within these lonely walls. It seemed very touching to see a human life stranded in such a beautiful but isolated spot, and I could not but wonder whether he was able all alone to keep up any fervency in his prayers, and whether he found it really any easier to be good than other men.

We have met lately some travellers who have given us news of the " Chicago party " at Jerusalem. You will remember that Mrs. Lee and her brother and his wife, Mr. and Mrs. Spafford, and a little band of followers started a fanatical mystical form of religion some years ago in Chicago, guided thereto, as they most fervently believed, by the Lord Himself, through a series of most remarkable signs. Mrs. Lee was the " Moses " of the New Dispensation, and Mrs. Spafford was " The Righteous Branch ", and others of their members were equally exalted personages ! Their fanaticism was simply unbounded,[1] but strange to say they were all of them people of education and intelli-gence, and of undoubted and unusual piety ; and

[1] H.W.S. wrote about this group of fanatics in *Religious Fanaticism*, Chapter VI. The original leader, she tells us, was a Mrs. Lee, " a charming lady, whose husband had held some official position in Washington ". After praying for some tangible sign, by which she might recognise the will of the Lord, Mrs. Lee was given, so she believed, such a sign, namely " that her lower jaw was cracked against her upper jaw with a loud crack ", whenever she was properly carrying out the Lord's will. Later, " as the cracking was very loud, it became unpleasant to her husband, especially as it would often take place in the very middle of a meal, so she prayed that the Lord would please give her a quieter sign " and it was graciously transferred " to her eyes, which were drawn back into her head, as if by strings fastened behind and pulled by an invisible hand ".

With such and other evidence of infallible direction, she had no difficulty in leading a number of disciples to Jerusalem, where they were disappointed of every promised and expected sign, a fact, it seems, by which they were not in the least disconcerted. Later Mrs. Lee was deposed, and another leader appointed in her place.

moreover they were all middle-aged ! . . . They had a great many remarkable " leadings "; and finally were called, as they believed, to Jerusalem there to await the manifestation of the " Branch ", (when) the Star of Bethlehem would come and rest on Mrs. Spafford's head. . . . Of course, nothing of the kind took place, but nothing daunted they have gone on.

To her friends

Aet. 54.

ROME, *April* 27, 1886

I give myself up as a hopeless case as regards the Old Masters. I *cannot* like them, try as hard as I may. There is certainly something wrong either with them or with me. Public opinion says it is with me, and so I suppose it must be ; but private conviction says it is with them. Well, I am sorry, but what *is* a body to do under the circumstances but just be honest and bear the consequences ?

I read and read about these pictures and try to work myself up all I can, but it will not work, and I have given up now in despair. We brought with us some little books of Ruskin's called " Mornings in Florence ", each one taking up some especial Church or picture, and telling you just when and how to see it, and what you ought to see in it. We determined to take one of them and follow its directions exactly, and see what would come of it. So we started out one morning for the Santa Croce Church.

Ruskin told us to walk straight up the aisle looking neither to the right nor the left, so we did. Then he told us to go into a little chapel to the right of the altar, so we did. Then he told us to stand still awhile until we got used to the dim light, so we did. Then he told

us to look at a fresco of Giotto's on the right of the
window, so we did. Then he told us to walk back
down the Church to where we would find two marble
tombstones laid in the pavement, so we did. And at
this point came a crucial moment; for of one of the
figures carved on these slabs, Ruskin says that if you
see nothing right and lovely and exquisite in this
sculpture, then you will see nothing in any Florentine
drawing or carving.

You can imagine with what fear and trembling I
turned my eyes downward upon this crucial tomb ! !
Suppose I did not like it, what was I to do ? Pack up
and leave Florence at once, as one unfit to tread its
artistic streets ? I held my breath in fear ! But in a
moment I breathed freely ! I found I *did* like and
understand the grace and beauty of the old tomb !
I might stay in Florence.

To her friends

Aet. 54.

VENICE, *May* 11, 1886

Of Carpaccio's " Presentation of the Virgin "
Ruskin says, " You may measure yourself outside and
in, your religion, your taste, your knowledge of art,
your knowledge of men and things, by the quantity
of admiration which honestly, after due time given,
you can feel for this picture " . . . We sat ourselves
down before it to measure ourselves at leisure, and
while on the whole I quite liked it, yet I fear my
measurement must be far short of Ruskin's standard.
But I do not feel discouraged, nevertheless, for there
is a picture of Tintoretto's called " Paradise " which
Ruskin says is the " thoughtfullest and mightiest
picture in the world ", and which is simply a great

cataract of human legs and arms and bodies and heads jumbled together in inextricable confusion—and if *that* is a sample of Ruskin's taste, I am thankful I do not measure up to his standard.

To her friends

Aet. 54.

DORKING, *Aug.* 1, 1886

I went to Dorking to join Lord and Lady Mount Temple at a friend's house there to meet Laurence Oliphant. He has been living in Palestine for several years, and actually owns the plain of Armageddon! His wife died lately, and he has come over to England on a mission to propagate a sort of mystic spiritualism of a most peculiar kind. It is set forth in a book he and his wife wrote in partnership, called " Sympneumata ".

The gist of it is that each one of us has a missing half in the spirit world which he calls our " Sympneuma " or " Counterpart ", and the great business of our souls ought to be to find this " Sympneuma " and come into union with it! He thinks this is the secret to regenerate the world!! I had expected of course that we were going to some fanatic's plain little house in the village of Capel, where I was told to leave the train, but instead I was met by a stylish footman and conducted to an elegant carriage and pair, in which I was taken to a most beautiful country place, where I found a grand dinner party!

After dinner Laurence Oliphant read us a long paper about " It " and " He ", of which I could make neither head nor tail, but I gathered that " It " meant the Sympneuma. It sounded like pure unadulterated trash! The next morning, however, he unfolded his ideas to me, and they were about as I tell you. I told him of the dangers I saw in his teachings, and illustrated what I had to say by the account of fanaticisms to which similar teaching had led a great many good people in America ; but I might as well have talked to the whirlwind. I am very glad, however, that I know what his teachings really are, as I can warn people more intelligently against them. It seems very sad to see such a really bright and good man so deluded. I cannot understand it at all.[1]

To her friends

BROADLANDS, *Aug.* 13, 1886

The visit of Lady Pembroke and her friends, Lady Lothian and Lady Brownlow, was, I suppose, a very fair sample of the way with such visitings among the aristocracy, and it was tiresome, I am sure, to everyone concerned. It appears to be the regular thing to take

---

[1] Readers of her *Religious Fanaticism* will recognise the moderation of this letter, for, as she there frankly reveals, Laurence Oliphant, together with his disciples, actually carried out, to the utmost possible extent, the practices of which Robert Pearsall Smith was suspected— even by the irreligious—of having only partially attempted : and this in spite of the fact that the prophet who taught these doctrines to Oliphant had swindled him out of a fortune in California, that state so strangely fecund in curious and profitable religions. At one time Laurence Oliphant and his wife carried on their work in Palestine. In the course of this work Mrs. Oliphant felt compelled into high-minded but unreticent intimacy with Arabs, " no matter ", as H.W.S. writes, " how degraded and dirty they were. It was," she goes on, " a great trial to her to do this, and she felt that she was performing a most holy mission. As she was one of the most refined and cultivated of English ladies, it is evident that nothing but a strong sense of duty could have induced her to such a course." In this last sentence, being written by the mother of Logan Pearsall Smith, we may allow ourselves, perhaps, to detect a grain of irony.

Oliphant openly propounded his preposterous doctrine to her. She expostulated with him, " although," as she writes, " I might as well have talked to Niagara ". (*Religious Fanaticism*, Chapter VIII.)

visitors first all over the show rooms of the house and descant on the pictures, statuary, etc., and then all over the gardens and as much of the park as they can drag themselves. So instead of sitting down and having a good talk, we all had to perform this painful duty. I confess I prefer my own way of having callers in my library at home, seated at my table with my " revolver " beside me, and my friends sitting in comfortable rocking-chairs before me. However, if I had Lady Pembroke and Lady Lothian and Lady Brownlow calling on me, I cannot tell what I might feel impelled to do ! It evidently was the conventional thing to go over the house and grounds, and no one seemed to think for a moment of doing anything else.

I frankly confess if I *lived* in England I should want to belong to the aristocracy.[1] My independent spirit would revolt, I fear, at the idea of having anyone Lord or Lady it over me. I always tell the aristocracy this, and they enjoy it greatly.

Archdeacon Sumner wore a black alpaca *apron* all the

[1] [According to her own words, this romance for the British aristocracy had started early, and—since fiction was frowned on—almost sinfully.]

" It was one ' First Day ' afternoon when there seemed to be nothing going on, I had borrowed a book from one of my schoolmates which she had told me was ' lovely ', and I took this book and a plate of apples and gingerbread, and stretched myself on the outside of my bed to read and eat at my leisure.

" The story I read that day, under these delightful circumstances, seemed to give me the nearest approach to perfect bliss of anything I had ever before experienced, and it remains in my memory as one of the happiest days of my life. The book was ' The Earl's Daughter ', by Grace Aguilar, and to my young American and Quaker mind an Earl was more like an archangel than a man, and to be an Earl's daughter was almost akin to being a daughter of heaven. And to this day, in spite of all the disillusions that life has brought me about earls and their daughters, the old sense of grandeur that filled my soul with awe on that First Day afternoon so long ago, never fails to come back for at least a moment when earls and countesses are mentioned in my presence." (*Unselfishness of God*, p. 129.) L.P.S.

time, and I was very anxious to know what it was for, so I asked him out plump and plain, to the great amazement of all the party. He said it was a remnant of the old cassock that the priests of Rome still wear, but I could not find out that it had any especial meaning. There was a High Church clergyman present who said they *ought* to be wearing the *whole* cassock, and that all Clergymen ought to wear it. These High Churchmen are a subject of great perplexity to me. How they can be as " High " as they are and not go over to Rome is incomprehensible to my uninitiated mind. But they all seem very holy men, and I expect our Father in Heaven does not mind *their* little notions any more than He minds *ours*, whether aprons or coats.

To her friends

Aet. 54.

LONDON, *Aug.* 26, 1886

On August 24th Mrs. Bottome and I went to the little dark barred-in cage reserved for women in the House of Commons. We heard both Parnell and Gladstone make long speeches, and *most* interesting ones. We both of us have heard so much said on the conservative side since we have been over here, that we felt rather shaky on the Home Rule question, but Parnell and Gladstone were too much for us, and we wheeled right over into their ranks. They talked like men who had justice and right on their side, and could afford to be calm and quiet about it.

Mrs. Bottome said she and I reminded her of a story she had heard of a mermaid who was turned into a beautiful princess and married a great king. She told the King she would be all right as long as she did

not see a stream or a lake, but that if that should ever
occur she could not answer for what she would do.
They lived very happily together for many months, and
the King carefully guarded his fair bride from seeing
any water. But one day he carelessly allowed the
coachman to drive them across a river. With a scream
of delight his bride made one spring into the water and
was lost to sight forever. Just so, Mrs. Bottome said,
she and I were all right as long as we were kept away
from the radical river, but the moment we caught sight
of it, with one leap we plunged in, and were happy
again in our native element.

To her daughter, Mary Costelloe (Berenson)
Aet. 54.

AT SEA, *Sept.* 23, 1886

* * * * * * * The above stars represent 7 days of
sea-sickness, which my pen refuses to chronicle. All
my Mind Cure for sea-sickness was a fancied dream !
But never mind, it is over now, and I am once more in
America, dear old free and unaristocratic and yet all
aristocratic America !

To her daughter, Mary Costelloe (Berenson)
Aet. 55.

GERMANTOWN, *Mar.* 25, 1887

If ever I am disabled, I want thee to remind me that
I have always declared my intention of being waited
on by hired help, and I want thee to insist that I shall
do it. When grandma was sick once I insisted on
her having a nurse very much against her will, in fact
I had the nurse in the next room with her bonnet off
and her white apron on, before I told grandma.
Grandma declared she would not have her, and I said,

H

" Mother, dear, thee will *have* to have her. Thy children insist on it." Then dear grandma gave up and afterwards told me that the nurse was the greatest possible comfort. In fact she did not want to let her go when she got well.

I hope I shall have the *sense* to remember all this when I get disabled, but if I don't, thee must remind me. It is perfect folly, and often worse than folly, for the relatives of an invalid to wear themselves out with the *physical* part of the nursing. They ought to keep themselves fresh and bright for the other part. Moreover, many a life has been wrecked by the strain, for a hired nurse has no strain of the sympathies, which is often the hardest part of it.

To her friends

Aet. 55.

LONDON, *May* 10, 1887

Lady Mount Temple and I went together to the Women's Jubilee Meeting at a large hall in Lambeth, called " The Old Vic ", really Victoria Hall. *Such* a meeting I never attended ! It was crowded—at least 3000 people they said, and most of them women and girls from the slums, with no ideas apparently of how to behave in a meeting. Whenever the music was the least lively, they all got up and danced up and down on their seats, and the effects of this great mass of women, babies and all, bobbing up and down, up and down, was indescribable. As to being heard, that was impossible, except when we fairly shrieked. Dear Lady Mount Temple, with her gentle patrician voice, was like the rustling of a violet in a thunderstorm. *I* managed to make them hear, and I made a right loyal speech, spite of my radical Americanism. I was sur-

prised to find how much I had to say on the subject
when once I began. I find my *feet* very inspiring.

To her friends

Aet. 55.

LONDON, *June* 1, 1887

On the 21st Gurney Barclay had a large Yearly
Meeting garden party at his beautiful place called
Knott's Green, about 20 miles from London. There I
met John Bright, who is an uncle of Gurney Barclay's.
I had a little talk with him about politics, and said how
interested all Americans were. " No, you are not,"
he said brusquely. " You only care about the Irish
vote ! " I ventured a little disclaimer, when he said,
with even more brusqueness, " All those resolutions
passed by your legislatures, and those meetings in
protest held by Mayors and Governors are only *bunkum*.
They don't mean anything but a bid for Irish votes ! "
Then he added in a lower voice—" It is all of a piece
with Gladstone's bunkum, and the rest of them."
I confess the old man seemed to me to be thoroughly
put out by America. He ventured no prophecies for
the future, and said no human being could tell. He
was furious at what he called Gladstone's " wicked
tactics of obstruction " over the Coercion Bill.

On Derby Day we drove out to Tooting to meet the
people returning from the races on Epsom Downs,
which is one of the London sights. We found the
streets lined with crowds who had assembled to see the
return ; and on Clapham Common hundreds of
carriages were stationed full of spectators.

All there is to see, however, is just crowds of wagons,
and stages, and drags, and dog-carts, and vehicles of
all sorts and descriptions, filled with racing men and

women, and the crowd of hangers on at the races, most of them half drunk, and many of them decorated with green or blue gauze streamers around their hats and bonnets, and with ridiculous little rag dolls and puppets stuck in their hat bands, blowing striped horns and squirting water out of penny squirts. These rag dolls and water squirts seemed to be the principal amusement, and the great aim was to get a chance to squirt the water into people's ears and necks. One man off the top of a coach squirted some right down Mary's neck as they passed. I confess I did not see anything that would have paid *me* for standing for hours on the side walk, as thousands of people evidently did. " Seeing the return from the Derby " is one of the famous dissipations of London life.

To her friends

Aet. 55.

LONDON, *June* 18, 1887

The other day I did a very frolicsome thing. I wanted to see something essentially English, and everyone said that the Ascot week was the very most characteristic thing I could possibly do. So my brother-in-law [1] and I decided to go out one day. It is really a week of races to which all the Royalties and Aristocracy go, taking country places all around the neighbourhood for the week or being entertained.

We did not care for the races, but for the people, and it certainly was a very Englishy sight. A great many of the Aristocracy had drags, immense sorts of omnibuses with seats on top, and on these seats the young ladies sat and entertained their beaux, and ate their luncheons. The " drags " were arranged all

[1] Dr. Thomas, of Baltimore.

along one side of the " Course ", and on the other side
were the Stands for the less fortunate spectators.
However, the Prince of Wales, who *always* attends, has
a large " Box ", as it is called, capable of holding
several hundred, and this was filled with a gorgeously
dressed assemblage.

The scene was like a flower garden because of the
beautiful toilettes of the ladies, and the many bright
colored parasols. But why they care to get together
in such crowds to see a few horses racing I *cannot*
imagine. The tumult on the betting ground was something dreadful, and my heart ached and ached to
think of the ruin to morals and fortunes that *must* follow.

It is evidently the proper thing for the English upper
classes to go to Races, and it is eminently respectable.
I do not think that is the case with us, is it ? I did not
consider that *I* was going to a Race, for *my* interest was
simply in seeing a characteristic bit of English life,
which could be seen nowhere else. On Whit Monday
I saw an English lower class crowd taking their holiday,
and at Ascot I saw a higher class crowd doing the same,
and I confess the principal difference between them
seemed to be only and altogether in their *dress*. I
wonder if Carlyle is right, and if we all went unclothed,
whether we would all be on an absolute equality ?

To her friends

Aet. 55.

LONDON, *July* 3, 1887

The great Jubilee took place, and it was truly a
wonderful affair. The whole nation seemed to go
wild over it, and I am strongly impressed with the
devotion of the English people of all grades and ranks
to the ranks above them. I believe the technical name

for this devotion is " snobbism ", and I have come to the conclusion that it is in the very atmosphere here, so that an Englishman, even the most radical, can no more help it than he can help breathing.   The crowds of people that stand craning their necks for hours just to catch a glimpse of some Royalty's bonnet or hat are both ridiculous and pitiful to see.   I myself believe that England is given over to snobbism and that no Radical party will have the slightest chance of success for many years to come, if ever again.

The Tories, who are the Aristocrats, have an immense majority, both in Parliament and out, and are carrying everything with a high hand, and mean to go on doing it, so that I can see no hope for Ireland, or for the poor man anywhere.   What is the most amazing thing is that the poorer classes themselves are all so largely Tory.   A little notice from an aristocrat reduces them to abject Toryism at once.

To her friends

Aet. 55.

LONDON, *July* 9, 1887

We found a crowded stream of elegantly dressed aristocracy ascending the stairs and being received by Sir Frederick Leighton, and then dispersing through the different galleries.   It was an interesting thing to get a peep at the Aristocracy in low necks and short sleeves, and pinched waists, but this very soon palled. Still there certainly *is* a charm about the English upper classes that is indescribable, and I confess I *do* enjoy them exceedingly.   For one thing they are far more like Americans than the classes below them.

I am quite convinced that we Americans are in a

further state of evolution than the English. What is rare with them is universal with us. And it delights me to see how they appreciate us. To be an American seems to be a certain passport to their favour. They seem to look on us all as belonging to the Aristocracy. And they sigh for our special developments of freedom, and largeheartedness and unconventionality, and spirit of progress. I do my best, you may be sure, to intensify this feeling of envy of our lot, and I especially make the English mouth water by my praises of the Women's Christian Temperance Union women and their work. I believe it would be very easy to make a " boom " for our women if they could be brought over here.

I have attended 2 meetings of Josephine Butler's on the subject of the infliction by England of the horrible C.D. Acts upon the women of the nations they conquer . . . My very soul blazed with indignation as I listened to the voiceless cry of my enslaved and outraged sisters of heathen lands ! I wonder God does not sweep England out of existence at one blow ! I cannot think that those old nations in the land of Canaan, the Hittites, and the Amorites, and the Perizzites, who were doomed to destruction because of their sins, *could* have been worse than England ! I tried to speak in one of those meetings, but broke down crying with an anguish of pity.

To her friends

Aet. 55.

LONDON, *July* 20, 1887

Madame Blavatsky is the great Leader of the Theosophical Society which believes in the occult teaching of the East, and which professes to be under the control and guidance of the Mahatmas or Adepts, who live in the hidden mountain fastnesses of Thibet, and who are supposed to have mastered the secrets of the control of spirit over matter. I have long wanted to see her, and one evening last week an intimate friend of hers took us out to her little cottage at Norwood, where she is writing a new book to be called " The Secret Doctrine ", that is to be three times as large as her immense book, " Isis Unveiled ". It is a history of all that is known of occultism from the earliest ages down to the present. (All that is known, and all that is *imagined* also I suspect.)

We found her at her table surrounded by books and papers smoking endless cigarettes, and looking like a perfect frump. She is enormously fat, and looks very coarse and shabby. I could not see how the ladies who were with me *could* kiss her. Neither could I understand how the intelligent cultured young men I met there could possibly bring themselves to be her disciples. Yet such they evidently were, attracted I concluded at last, by the high ideal of purity and self-sacrifice she has incorporated in her doctrines, whether she practises them or not.

All sorts of stories are circulated concerning Mme. Blavatsky, such as that she is hundreds of years old, and has kept herself alive by the occult secret, that she can work miracles, that she has visits from Indian " Mahatmas " who transport themselves through the air from their hidden mountain haunts in Thibet, etc. etc. All which rubbish seems perfectly ridiculous in the presence of a fat old woman, with blowsy hair, and racked with rheumatism, dressed in a dirty gown and smoking endless cigarettes which she continually makes for herself.

The Psychical Society sent out a delegate to India to investigate Her so-called miracles, and proved with absolute satisfaction to themselves that they were all stupendous frauds, but of course her followers have explanations which are equally satisfactory to them. I confess she impressed me as a sincere but deluded woman, very much like the deluded fanatics of different sorts with whom we are so familiar in America.

Among other things Mme. Blavatsky believes in evolution through repeated incarnations, and when I asked her what would happen to her in case she should die that same night, she gravely informed me that she would have to look out for a new body in which to be reincarnated, and that the way would be to catch someone just at the point of death, and slip into their body just at the moment that they slipped out ! ! She said she should choose a young boy about 16 or so, as she had had enough of being a woman !

I was struck dumb at finding that her followers present received this statement in perfect faith ; and I actually had not my wits sufficiently collected to pursue my inquiries as to how things would go on afterwards etc. etc. Could anything more absurd be imagined ? And yet one man of evident culture and intelligence present said in response that he had always thought that Beethoven must have slipped himself in this way into Wagner's body at some moment when Wagner had been very ill and had slipped out. Let us hope poor Wagner had no intention of returning himself ! Suffice it to say, I did not join the Theosophical Society *that* evening !

To her friends

Aet. 55.

LONDON, *Aug.* 1887

Most of the guests gathered at Broadlands on the 2nd of August. There were about 40 entertained in the house, about 20 clergymen, and when you understand that each person had a room to themselves, and that some of the ladies had maids, who had also to be accommodated besides all the house-servants, and the family, you can get a little idea of the number of rooms the house contains. Someone told me it was 100, and I can easily believe it.

George Macdonald and his wife were there, Canon Wilberforce, Lord Radstock, Mr. Clifford,[1] Lady Darnley, etc. etc., I cannot give all the names. Our days were divided as follows. Breakfast at 9. Family Prayers at 10, followed by ½ hour's talk on thoughts suggested by the leader of Prayers. Meeting under the Beeches at 11. Lunch at 1. Meeting under the Beeches or in the Orangery at 2. Afternoon tea at 5. A reading in the dining-room, generally by George Macdonald at 6, while Lord Radstock and others held an Evangelistic meeting for the people of Romsey under the Beeches. Dinner at 8. Family prayers again at 9.30. Bed at 10.

After we had separated for the night downstairs, each with our candle presented to us by the solemn looking butler, there always began a visitation in wrappers from room to room, when confidences were exchanged, and troubles poured out, and perplexities

---

[1] Edward Clifford, for many years a prominent worker with the Church Army. He was a talented painter who imitated, and sometimes copied, Burne-Jones. These copies, it has been said, were hard or impossible even for experts to distinguish from original works of the master.

aired, so that it was generally pretty late before one really got to bed.

To M.

Aet. 55.

BALTIMORE, Oct. 28, 1887

Tonight Miss Willard is to speak. There are 13 of us staying at Aunt Mary's. Imagine 13 " earnest " women in one house !

To Mrs. Henry Ford Barclay

Aet. 55.

PHILADELPHIA, Oct. 31, 1887

We came into lodgings (on our return from England) because we found that Logan had decided, with our approval, to give up business and devote himself to a literary life.[1] He had faithfully tried business life for a year, and had been very successful in it, and was on the sure road to make a fortune. But he said the impulse was so strong within him towards a literary life that he could not resist it, and he would rather be a poor Professor with just enough to live on very moderately, than the wealthiest business man living.

Of course we could not feel it right to withstand so strong an impulse and conviction, and moreover both his father and I agreed in feeling it was really the right thing, especially as he will we trust always have a moderate competence from the family property. He has therefore given up his position, and is now with us,

---

[1] Readers of Logan Pearsall Smith's *Unforgotten Years* will know that, in his escape from business, his mother took a more conscious and diplomatic—one might almost say a more cunning—part than she here admits to. (*Unforgotten Years*, Chapter V, " Business and Release ".)

studying under a private tutor to prepare himself for Oxford in the spring. With Mary and Logan both in England, and Alys very desirous of studying there also as soon as she is through College here,[1] we have decided to make England our home for the next few years though we shall not go to housekeeping there at once, as we would rather keep ourselves free to move about with Logan or Alys. When parents have only 3 children as we have, we feel as if we must keep close to them, and the new baby[2] is an immense attraction. I have so many dear friends in England that I feel almost as much at home there as here. I have always had a sort of feeling that sometime I would live in England, and I feel that it is all in the Divine ordering, and am very happy in the prospect.

To M.

Aet. 56.

PHILADELPHIA, *Feb.* 5, 1888

I have had my black plush made into a Princess with a trail, and shall wear that at the wedding and feel like a slave in it.

To Miss Priscilla Mounsey

Aet. 56.

PHILADELPHIA, *Feb.* 19, 1888

People that get *too* resigned generally become chronic invalids, and that is vigorously to be avoided. I have made up my mind to go on until I drop in the traces, as long as I can put one foot before the other.

---

[1] Alys graduated 1890. L.P.S.
[2] Ray Costelloe, who afterwards married Mr. Oliver Strachey, brother of Lytton Strachey.

VII

PLEASURES AND PALACES

To her friends

Aet. 56.

On my crossing from America Mrs. Brooks completely saddled herself on me. She had her chair put beside mine on deck and considered herself to be " under my wing ", as she expressed it. I am afraid she found it a wing of marble. I could not gush with her worth a cent.

I do not find that I feel myself to be any different as an English subject than as an American. I have not the vote in either place, so I am not a citizen of either, and have no call to be patriotic. In fact, I do not see how *women* can ever feel like anything but aliens in whatever country they may live, for they have no part or lot in any, except the part and lot of being taxed and legislated for by men. You need not think, therefore, that I feel any pangs in leaving America as far as my country is concerned. I do regret very greatly leaving so many dearly loved friends, but I feel as if I should see you all often after all, and we are not separated in spirit.

Mary's daughter, Ray, my first grandchild, is the sweetest little thing that ever was. She sleeps all night like a softly breathing seraph, and when I wake I hear her little rustlings like a tiny bird in its nest. My spectacles charmed her at once, and in a few minutes after we first met we were intimate friends, and in an incredibly short space of time we assumed our proper positions of mistress and slave. When I tell you that she sucks my watch and uses my spectacles as a hammer, you will understand which one of us is mistress, and which the slave ! She is in short a perfectly delicious baby, and I am a perfectly idiotic grandmother !

To her friends
Aet. 56.

TORQUAY, *June* 10, 1888

As usual Lady Mount Temple is full of interesting things, and to-day she introduced me to a mysterious creature, a *man* he looked like, who is the leader of a strange sect called the " Temple ", and who declared to me that he had not slept a wink for 8 years, but had every night got out of his body and travelled around the world on errands of service for the Lord ! ! He declared that he sees angels as plainly as he sees men, and knows them all apart, and that Michael has light flaxen hair, and Gabriel dark eyes and hair, and they all live in the sun ! But I cannot begin to repeat all his nonsense. He was like all other cranks with some slight variations, and like all the rest believes that his religion and his experiences are the ushering in of a new era in the world's history. I wonder how many " new eras " I have heard tell of ? At least 50 I should think. And meanwhile the old world wags on just as it has always done, and will wag, I suspect, in spite of all their new eras.

Another very interesting thing has been a visit we paid to a very mysterious brother and sister who had lived in a little shut-in cottage on the side of the cliff for 25 years, and during all that time had never made a single friend in all the neighbourhood, and had never had a single visitor in their house as far as anyone could tell. Why they had kept themselves so secluded no one could say. Lady Mount Temple with her tender sympathy for all who are in trouble, had gone to see them when she first went to Babba-combe and somehow found her way into their hearts, but even now, though it has been many years, she knows nothing of their story. The brother paints and the sister plays on the harp, and their little shut-in grounds are radiant with flowers. They keep no servant, and no workman ever enters their place.

To her daughters

Aet. 56.

LLEWYN BARRIED, RHAYADER VALLEY,
NR. LLANDRINDOD WELLS [1]

Aug. 8, 1888

I wish you would pay off all our calls while I am away from Wales. DO ! There are six to pay. You can go in detachments. Let me be spared any further sacrifices in this line. I have brought a novel to read called " Cut by the County " with which I shall arm myself against the next County we live in. I cannot help hoping that the next place we live in the County will not call on us, for I must say it is a decided bother. For me, in my old age, to begin *paying calls* is a little too much to ask, after all my lifetime testimony against it.

[1] In the summer of 1888 Robert Pearsall Smith rented a country house in the Rhayader Valley—Shelley's valley—near Llandrindod Wells. L.P.S.

To her friends

Aet. 56.

LONDON, *Jan.* 1889

Lady Tavistock is a most charming person and evidently very religious. She arranged with me for an interview of herself and Mrs. Benson, the wife of the Bishop [Archbishop] Benson who lives in Lambeth Palace, on the subject of my views on holiness and the life of faith. It is to come off this week.

Lady Tavistock and Rachel Fowler and I are hoping to start some Ladies' Prayer meetings in London during the " Season ", for the upper class ladies, who, Lady Tavistock says, are starving for some food outside of their Churches, where often they are fed with the merest chaff. Lady Tavistock is really the Marchioness of Tavistock, and her husband is the heir to the Duke of Bedford, so anything she starts is sure to go, and she seems especially fitted for just such a meeting, as she has had a great deal of success among her own tenants at " Oakley House " in Bedford, and is a most devoted Christian. It is very interesting to see so many really earnest Christians among the very highest nobility, but I must confess, it is mostly among the women.

To her friends

Aet. 57.

ROME, *Feb.* 7, 1889

It is my 57th birthday to-day, and I am *delighted* to be growing older.

I am convinced it is a great art to know how to grow old gracefully, and I desire to practise it. One secret of it I am sure is to *take the side* of the young people, and

I mean to do this just as far as possible. When I remember my own youth, and recall the immense power any old person, who believed in me and sympathised with me, had over me in those days, I cannot but think my influence for good over the young people of my day will be far greater by the road of sympathy than by the road of antagonism.

The next thing I want to say is that it is worth living 57 years just to be the grandmother of such a delicious little granddaughter as my little Ray Costelloe ! I have often thought at different periods of my life that I had at last found my proper niche, but now I am convinced my proper niche is being a *grandmother*, I fit into it so completely, and enjoy it so thoroughly ! If becoming a grandmother was only a matter of choice I should advise everyone of you straightway to become one. There is no fun for old people like it !

Rome is full of priests in all their varied and picturesque dresses and I confess it does give me solid satisfaction to see *men* obliged to walk around in this muddy Rome with long flapping skirts twisting around their ankles at every step ! It seems to introduce a little more fairness into things.

To Lady Mount Temple and Mrs. Russell Gurney [1]

Aet. 57.

FRIDAY'S HILL[2], *Oct.* 3, 1889

I think of you now as two " enchanted Princesses " sitting in a bower of heavenly love, while I feel *myself*

[1] Mrs. Russell Gurney, Lady Mount Temple and H.W.S. formed themselves as a holy band of " Trins " comparable to the five mystic birds of Philadelphia long before (see *ante*). L.P.S.

[2] In 1889 my father rented Friday's Hill House and estate, at Fernhurst, Sussex, near Haslemere, Surrey. It now seems to me odd that

to be a sort of humdrum mortal plodding along in the common paths, with packing to do, and cooks to interview and workmen to oversee, and all sorts of mundane affairs to attend to. But after all I am just as truly dwelling in fairyland as when with you, for our true and only fairyland is the beloved and beautiful will of God, which environs us all everywhere and in everything.

To her daughter, Mary Costelloe (Berenson) [1]

Aet. 58.

44 GROSVENOR ROAD, LONDON
March 15, 1890

When Ray comes in to breakfast in the morning her first proceeding is to run round the table telling me to say, " Who is that frisking around the table ? " To this grandpa has to answer, " I guess it is a calf." Then she says to me, " You are the mamma cow and you must call your little calf to breakfast." Then I have to say, " Come little calf, come to breakfast." Then she trots over and gets in her chair beside me and says, " Here the calf is sitting on its tail, and you are the mamma cow sitting on your tail." And so she goes on all through breakfast. She is *too* bewitching. Yesterday when she was in here she asked me towards the last whether I was going to give her a chocolate when she

---

I, who was then at Oxford, should have insisted on a house with woods and shooting for our summer and autumn abode. The " Old Adam " of sport in me was completely baffled by the Sussex poachers and soon died a natural death. L.P.S.

[1] Early in 1890 H.W.S.'s daughter, Mrs. Costelloe, went to Florence to study Italian Art under the tutorship of Mr. Bernard Berenson, whom she married (1900) a year after the death of her husband B. F. C. Costelloe. In the intervening period she stayed in Florence, with only occasional visits home, while her two daughters lived with their father at 41 Grosvenor Road, only three doors off from the home of H.W.S. at No. 44. L.P.S.

went home. I said " Yes ". She was silent for a minute or two, and then said, " I hear God's voice saying it is time for me to go home now ! ! " I could not help thinking she was not so unlike some older Christians, who hear God's voice telling them to do what they have already set their hearts on doing !

To-day Ray pretended I was the devil and she gave me her naughty children who would not take their hot baths quietly to burn up.

To her friends

Aet. 58.

LONDON, *April* 1890

I went with Lady Henry Somerset to see the Salvation Army Shelters, and it was one of the saddest and most discouraging sights we had either of us ever seen, not so much because of the poverty, as because of the plain and unmistakable signs of degradation from drink. I never saw a more beastly set of human beings, and it seems an insult to beasts to call them this. For a penny these sots, for they were nothing else, could get a decent place to sleep, in a comfortable airy room, and for another penny they could get enough to eat. . . . They were all evidently professional tramps, and they could " bum " around all day in their haunts of drink and vice, sure at night of a warm and comfortable shelter and good food for the infinitesimal sum of 2*d*. If one enjoyed bumming nothing could be more satisfactory.

Nearly all the Christian workers among the slums feel grave doubts of the wisdom of these Salvation Army Shelters, as they find by experience that all such things only encourage thriftlessness and pauperise the recipients. No doubt some do get converted at the meetings, and that of course is pure gain. But the night we were there it seemed hopeless to expect to reach such a sodden set of drunkards.

Lady Henry Somerset to Hannah Whitall Smith

LONDON, *Dec.* 17, 1890

It was such a joy to see thee. I wish I could tell how much thee is to my life. I always turn to thee as a sort of rest and often just think about thy face when I get troubled. I am not very good at saying all I feel, but deep down I do feel it all so much.

To her friends

Aet. 59.

SYRACUSE, SICILY, *Feb.* 26, 1891

The excursion of all excursions we took on the 20th to Segesta and Selinunte. It rained when we started, and it snowed, and rained, and hailed, and blew, in alternate snatches all the day through.

Such mud and such a climb I hope never to encounter again during all the span of my natural life. Details would be harrowing ; so suffice it to say after climbing for endless miles upon miles, as it seemed to me, though really I believe it was only a climb of $\frac{3}{4}$ of an hour, we suddenly turned the corner of a cliff, and there before us standing in lonely grandeur, on the summit of a smooth grassy hill, surrounded by mountains on every side, was the Temple of Segesta ! It seemed utterly alone somehow, as though it belonged to a different world from ours ; and after our weary toilsome climb, it looked so profoundly still and at peace. But the wind whistled through the columns, and gusts of snow and rain

blinded us, and we were fairly *driven* away long before
we had half exhausted our enjoyment of all the grandeur
and beauty of the place. Then came the journey back
to the carriage, with that dreadful river to cross.

How differently people can look at things ! At
table-d'hôte a gentleman sitting next to me, whom I
had met among the ruins of Segesta during the day,
said in a most lugubrious tone—" How solemn these
ruins are ! How deeply they make us feel that we are
nothing but poor worms of the dust, here to-day and
to-morrow gone into oblivion." " Oh, dear no," I
replied most cheerfully, " that is not the way they make
me feel at all. They fill me with joy to think that we
ourselves are so much grander than the things we make,
that the earth which holds them cannot hold us, and
that we are like birds, alighting here for a moment and
then stretching our wings to fly off to a better world."
I never felt so *immortal* as I have since I came among
these crumbling ruins.

Here we met a Mr. Dennis who has excavated a
great deal at Cyrene in North Africa, and owns a ruined
Temple there which, now that he is old, he will be glad
to sell to anyone who is ambitious of becoming the pro-
prietor of a ruined Grecian Temple. A few years
since I am certain I should have wanted to purchase it
myself, if I could have afforded it. I remember I
purchased a little lake in Florida with 80 acres around
it for the sake of owning the alligator that lived in the
lake ; and I purchased a claim in Wyoming for the sake
of owning some land in a state where women had the
vote ; and why not have added a ruined Greek Temple
to the collection ?

On the 9th we went to Capri, and from there we took
a sail boat across to Sorrento, where we slept. That
sail boat was a rash proceeding on my part ! But the

sea looked smooth, and the day was lovely, and the
distance looked insignificant, and my usual good sense
seemed to desert me, and we did the foolish thing.
Alys enjoyed it, but I suffered.   It took us 3 hours, and
the smooth sea proved to be full of unsuspected hills and
hollows, and I found myself feeling more and more
" meachin ", and could only console myself by saying
over and over inwardly with continually increasing
emphasis, " Never again, *Never* again *Never* NEVER
NEVER again ! ! "

It is a delightful feeling to find one's self gradually
getting *done* with this world.   It seems such an assurance
or prophecy of the better country, that is the heavenly,
towards which one is gradually drawing nigher and
nigher.   Not that I have any immediate prospect of
getting there, but I do like to feel that I have begun to
pack up to go.   So I have said farewell to Sicily and the
Temples with a happy heart, and have turned my face
homeward without one longing look behind.

To her friends

Aet. 59.

LONDON, *May* 4, 1891

London is in the full tide of the " May Meetings ",
and I will just give you my list of engagements for this
week, so as to give you a little idea of all that I am
drawn into doing.

Monday, May 4th. *Morning*. Visit from Lady
Tollemache to talk of spiritual things. *Afternoon*. Go
with Alys and Lady Albinia [Hobart] to see Lady
Henry Somerset about Girls' Clubs. *Evening*.
National Temperance League Anniversary.

Tuesday, May 5th. Visit to Mrs. A. B. who is in
spiritual trouble and wants help. *Afternoon*. Bible

Reading at Brixton. *Evening*. Reception for Temperance Women.

Wednesday, May 6th. *Morning*. British Women's Temperance Association Temperance Meeting. *Afternoon*. 2.30 Moral Reform Union Meeting. 3.30 Meeting about Women Guardians. *Evening*. Jerusalem Medical Mission to Women.

Thursday, May 7th. *Morning*. Suffrage Meeting. *Afternoon*. Tea with Lady Pease. *Evening*. Speak at Polytechnic to a Girls' Club.

Friday, May 8th. *Morning*. Shopping. *Afternoon*. Bible Reading in Highbury. *Evening*. Dine Lady Mount Temple's.

Saturday, May 9th. Go to Bristol to give a Bible Reading.

I wonder how many of our tombstones will have to be inscribed with the epitaph " Died of too many Meetings " ?

To her daughter, Mary Costelloe (Berenson)

Aet. 59.

FRIDAY'S HILL, *Aug.* 16, 1891

Logan is making some Pot-pourri with rose leaves, and I gave Ray some old roses to pull to pieces to go into the pot.   When it was all done, she said very complacently, " Won't Uncle Logan be pleased? Won't he kiss his little Ray and hug her for giving him so many rose leaves? "   I answered mechanically " Yes ", and she went on talking about it for a little, repeating over and over how her Uncle Logan *would* hug and kiss her ; and then she said in entirely a different tone of voice, " Grandma, you and I *believe* this about Uncle Logan, but we *know* he won't do it at all, don't we? "   Was it not a subtle distinction ?

Of course I love thee as much as thee loves Ray.   But I cannot have her all to myself, and my very love teaches me to stand on one side and take such scraps as I can get.   Some day thee will understand this too, when Ray gives herself to some awful man !

To her friends

Aet. 59.

FRIDAY'S HILL, *Oct.* 5, 1891

We have been to see our neighbour at Blackdown, Lord Tennyson,[1] who is now 83 years of age.   I have always been devoted to his " In Memoriam " but I find that it is not the fashion with the most artistic young people of the present generation to admire Tennyson. They even declare he is not a poet in the true sense of the word at all !   I should be dreadfully shocked at this, only that I remember how in my young days *I* scorned the poetry which the generation before me admired, such as Cowper and Dryden, and even, I almost tremble to say it, Milton, who was never a poet to me.

The poets admired by the young people now are Shelley and Keats and Wordsworth and William Morris and Shakespeare.   Even Browning and Swinburne have gone out of fashion.   I cannot keep up with the coming generation in their literary taste, but it is very interesting to hear all about it.   And I confess I

[1] The Pearsall Smiths had first got to know Tennyson through a letter of introduction given by Walt Whitman to the daughters Mary and Alys, who had paid him a visit on the Isle of Wight.   Near his Sussex residence, it is said that Tennyson would walk on Blackdown, conspicuous with his cloak and beard and broad-brimmed hat ; if spectators appeared, he would angrily take cover behind bushes ; if no spectator turned up, he would, in still worse a temper, go back home, disappointed.

enjoy seeing them have opinions of their own. The individual human being is a wonderful thing to my mind, and everything that reveals it interests me immensely.

VIII

"THE EARL'S DAUGHTER"

To her friends

Aet. 59.

YONKERS, NEW YORK, *Oct.* 19, 1891

Thus far Lady Henry [Somerset] is charmed with America, except the streets and roads. These horrify her. They even shock me after the English ones. In New York we had to drive to her banker in William Street, and we were jolted so unmercifully that I do not believe Lady Henry will ever be willing to drive through the New York streets again. The roads here are not much better. She is amazed we stand it, and I confess I am too. She says everything looks as if it were only just begun.

To her family

Aet. 59.

NEW YORK, *Oct.* 26, 1891

After the meeting Olive [Seward] took us to the White House to call on Mrs. Harrison, and to see the President's weekly reception. Loyalty would demand that I should draw a veil over the President's wife, but the truth may as well be told. The poor dear Presidentess is not a Lady, and she neither acted nor looked like one. She was dressed in an old done-up black silk made in the fashion of about 10 years ago, and apparently pieced out with all sorts of odds and ends of silk. She called Lady Henry " Miss Somerset ", and then feeling that was not right, she called her " Miss

Lady ". She had a strong Western accent and said " Yes Ma'am " with a dreadful twang on the *ma'am*. She displayed the utmost ignorance of affairs, and seemed to be a woman utterly without culture in any direction. It was a sample of American democracy that I could have willingly withheld from Lady Henry's inspection, but it certainly was an experience.

After seeing the Presidentess we went into the President's public reception which he holds every Wednesday, and which is free to every human being, rich or poor, old or young, black or white, who may choose to come. It was a sight to be seen for English eyes, and Lady Henry was delighted with it. It was the most beautiful illustration of the true Democracy of our country possible. There in the Executive Mansion of the great American nation stood the President of that nation shaking hands with anyone who chose to come, all received on a perfect equality, and all as free of the said mansion as though it were their own home. Some of the groups who passed through were poor families with the father carrying the baby and the next older child clinging to the mother's skirts. Then there were working men with their stained and frayed coats, and working women with their shabby waterproofs and their brown paper parcels, strangers and home folks, all sitting on the White House sofas and easy chairs, and walking at will about the rooms. It seemed incredible to English eyes, but Lady Henry delighted in it, and for my part I felt proud of a country where such a thing could be. . . .

It was still raining when we crossed over from Jersey City, and Lady Henry was *disgusted*, as well she might be, with the whole arrangements at that miserable Desbrosses St. ferry. I never knew before how disgraceful, and I think I may say with Papa, how *morti-*

fying that ferry is.   I wonder the New Yorkers stand it.
And yet when I see the condition of their streets I do not
wonder either, for I should say their streets had not
been touched since they were first made one hundred
years ago.   It is like driving over the rocky bed of a
stream and nearly jolts you to pieces. . . .

On Friday a grand " White Ribbon " [1] lunch was
given us.   The table cloth was trimmed with white
satin ribbons, all the flowers were white rosebuds, the
rolls were tied around with white ribbons, and at each
of our plates were bunches of white roses, tied together
with broad white ribbons on which our respective
names were painted with gilt paint.

We sat at that lunch table 2 mortal hours, and went
deliberately through the following 14 courses, with the
plates changed each time.   1. Raw oysters on half
shell.   2. Beef tea in cups.   3. Celery and radishes.
4. Lobster cutlets.   5. Salted almonds and olives.   6.
Ice cream in fancy little ice cups.   7. Chicken cutlets
and peas.   8. Celery and radishes again.   9. Large
cups of chocolate and whipped cream.   10. Salted
almonds and olives again.   11. Fancy ice creams and
cakes.   12. Salades and cheese.   13. Candies.   14.
Fruit.

Although the lunch was at 2.30 we had all the
windows shut in dark, and curtains drawn and candles
lighted.   This seems to be the New York fashion.   All
the grand people, Vanderbilts etc. are still out of town,
so we have not been entertained by any of them,
although they have offered their empty houses and
their horses and carriages for our use. . . .   On Saturday
the Council of the King's Daughters gave us a breakfast
at a famous up-town restaurant, like Delmonico's only

[1] The American White Ribbon corresponded to the English Blue
Ribbon of temperance.

more fashionable. This was very interesting as they are all most lovely and interesting women. Of course both at the White Ribbon lunch and the King's Daughters breakfast Lady Henry was perfectly charming and everybody fell in love with her. She was by far the prettiest and most charming woman at either of them, and by far the best dressed.

To her daughter, Mary Costelloe (Berenson)
Aet. 59.

GERMANTOWN, *Nov.* 7, 1891

Lady Henry Somerset and I have had a miserable voyage, no great storms but oh ! such sickness. I had had my bed made more comfortable so that I *could* lie in it, but my state-room was at the bow and tossed up and down like a rubber ball. I thought I was the biggest fool in creation for having come. I would like to say " Never again ", but the recollection of past similar remarks restrains me !

All the way out to Chicago I was trembling in my shoes in regard to the meeting of Lady Henry and Miss Willard. I had said so much to Lady Henry about Miss Willard that I began to ask myself, " suppose she should be disappointed ", and as I had not seen Frances for 4 or 5 years, I could not tell but she might have changed. But I need have had no fears for she was more charming than ever.

I notice what thee says about religion and there is much truth. All the surface part of religion, that is all the spectacular part and the emotional part are largely matters of geography and of race, and also I would say of era too. But behind and beneath all these there is a knowledge of God that must be and that is more or less the same everywhere. I like Jukes's illustration taken from the description of the Holy City in Revelation. The city lieth " foursquare " and has gates on every side. Consequently people who enter it come from all the four corners of the earth and travel in four opposite directions. The man who enters one gate must travel south while the man who enters the opposite gate must travel north. But all enter the city and meet there. And just so in finding God. We may travel on exactly opposite pathways according to our race, or country, or era, but we all meet in God at last. I fully agree with thee about the ticklishness of our emotions, and therefore that gate of entrance would never be the one for me, although I believe many do enter there.

To her friends

Aet. 59.

BOSTON, *Nov.* 10, 1891

It is almost impossible to get time to write in the *whirl* of a W.C.T.U.[1] Convention. Lady Henry and I are great " lions " in addition to all else, and this involves a lot of social work in the way of calls etc. that is more fatiguing even than meetings and Committees. Of course it is all her *title*, not to say that we neither of us have personal charms. But one's charms are greatly enhanced by the " Lady " that accompanies them. . . . This last week has been a tornado ! The Convention and the women have absorbed every second of our time. I have my hands full in guarding poor Lady Henry who is beset on every hand. *Everybody* wants to shake hands with her, and when she is tired I simply will not allow it. It is a battle to get

---

[1] Women's Christian Temperance Union.

her out of every meeting. I have to pull both her and Frances [Willard] out by main force. . . . I am looking longingly towards home and shall be delighted to get there. The women are lovely but there are a great many of them, and it is very tiring. Sixty pulpits were filled by our women on Sunday, and I preached 3 times. Lady Henry's Sermon was a great success.[1] The crowds were something fearful. She sent me ahead . . . and came later herself, and she was nearly torn to pieces getting through the crowd. She has a perfect ovation everywhere. Of course she is so lovely that all hearts are captured.

To her friends

Aet. 59.

BOSTON, *Nov.* 20, 1891

I do not believe any public character has ever come to America before who has aroused such enthusiastic love as she has. It is no sinecure to be her protector against her admirers. I have to guard her as a hen guards its chickens from the hawks, or she would be simply crushed with kisses, and handshakes, and birth-day books, and every other form of admiration possible. I tell her she *must* put on a stern front when I am gone, and learn how to protect herself. But she is so gracious and kindly, just like our sweet Lady Mount Temple, that it is hard for her to turn a cold shoulder to anyone.

---

[1] Lady Henry Somerset was a successful preacher, overcoming the prejudices even of those who were predisposed against her. Logan Pearsall Smith used to repeat a story of hers. She had been preaching at a town somewhere in the north of England ; when she had done, the mayor got up and said, " I am bound to confess that, although I have always disapproved of ladies appearing in public, I have examined her Ladyship closely and observed nothing *ondacent,* either in word or in gesture."

To her friends

Aet. 61.

FRIDAY'S HILL, *Sept.* 11, 1893

Beds in England as a general thing leave much to be desired. I have been to stay at fine places over here, where money seemed to flow like water, and have scarcely been able to sleep a wink because of the miserable bed. And the wife of one of England's greatest Lords, who had lived all her life in Castles, told me the other day that she had never had a comfortable bed in all her life until within the last year!

We have had another most beloved and honoured guest since I wrote my last Letter, and that is George Macdonald who came with his wife and two daughters. He is the dearest old man, so gentle and yet so strong, and with such a marvellous insight into spiritual things. He is like an old patriarch who embraces the whole world as his family, and spreads hands of blessing over all. He reminds me more of my own dear father than anyone else I ever met. But he has been very ill and seems much more feeble than I have ever known him. *He* thinks he has a slight stroke of paralysis, but his wife will not listen to this, and says it has only been nervous prostration from overwork. I expect, however, that he is growing old like some of the rest of us, and there is nothing to grieve over in this. He has done a beautiful work in the world, and it is only fair that now he should have a little prospect of rest.

There is something lovely to me in the gradual laying down of burdens and of responsibilities that is the privilege of growing old, combined with the happy outlook towards the glorious future. The only thing that is unlovely in old age to my mind is when it tries to hold on to its vanishing rights and responsibilities, and interferes with the free development of the generation that is called in the Divine order to take its place.

K

IX

THE GRANDMOTHER

To her friends

Aet. 61.

Oct. 17, 1893

It is lovely having Frances Willard in one's house. She is really the most charming and delicious of women, something absolutely unique in woman-kind, or man-kind either. I cannot describe what her charm is, but it arises partly, I am sure, from the singular simplicity of her nature, and the other-world way in which she looks at everything. She realises more than anyone I ever knew one's idea of being " seated in Heavenly places ", without, however, the slightest trait of a morbid religiousness, or of dogmatic assertion. Her optimism is perfectly contagious. She believes that God is in the world He has made, and that, in spite of all the " seemings " to the contrary, He is working out for the whole human race a glorious destiny when all sin shall be done away, and every sinner shall be brought into conformity with the image of Christ, and shall be made one with Him.

To her friends

Aet. 62.

LONDON, *Jan.* 20, 1894

I always feel content when I get a chance to sow a seed of thought in anyone's mind, even though they may at first reject it ; because I am sure, if it is a seed that has any life in it, it will be sure to germinate and grow and bear fruit sometime. I have had many seeds sown in my own soul that I rejected at first with scorn or horror, which however, have found a lodgement in spite of me, and which afterwards have brought forth an abundant harvest, to my own great surprise.

We have had a most interesting meeting here on Women's Trade Unions, addressed by Miss Clementina Black. I was Chairman, and made my maiden Trade Union speech on opening. Little did I think twenty years ago that I should ever find myself making a speech in favour of Trade Unions! But this is only another illustration of the growth and spread of ideas. And one of my objects in writing about it all is to sow some seeds in some of your minds, that will sooner or later bring forth the same fruit as has been brought forth in mine.

You may remember in one of my late letters my telling you about the great coal strike, and the victory of the miners on the principle of the " living wage ". Some extracts from this letter were printed in the Union Signal, and as a result I have a letter from a Tory lady, whose views are such a good illustration of the sort of arguments the " Classes " use, that I will send you a few extracts. She says she was greatly grieved at seeing my letter, and adds—" I know that the living wage means in the minds of the miners, champagne, hot beef soup, prime joints, immense waste in bread, cold meat thrown away, and above all plenty of gambling.

" I admit there was suffering during the strike, but it was all brought on by the Leaders of the Unions, who get large salaries and live on the fat of the land, and who are obliged to order strikes every little while in order to justify their continuance in office. These wicked men are covetous and ambitious, and line their own pockets at the expense of their misguided followers. The miners had no cause of complaint. In fact I know for a certainty that they often drive to the Pit's mouth in cabs. All this agitation is only got up to create a bitter feeling in the minds of the poor against the rich ; and I am sorry to see that *you* endorse it."

You can see from this letter how little the working people have to hope from the upper classes, who will persist in believing and declaring, as this lady does, that the bloated poor man lives on champagne and beef, and rides to his work in cabs ! You can make no headway against such pigheadedness !

To her friends

Aet. 62.

LONDON, *March* 16, 1894

The coming generation are not going to see things as we have seen them, that is very clear ; and the food that has satisfied us will not satisfy them. But this does not trouble me. *We* did not see things as the generation before us did. We *could not*, as each one of us individually knows, and we must let this make us tolerant of the generation that is to follow us.

And one thing is very manifest, and that is that this coming generation is inspired with very high ideals and is filled with a generous impulse for the uplifting of humanity that is far ahead of what was known when we were young. If I were to express the difference broadly, I think I would say that our great concern in those days was to save our own souls, while the great concern of the coming generation now is to save the souls of others. By " saving the soul " I do not mean only a saving that is to affect eternity, but the saving that affects life now and here—that makes out of human beings good men and women, good citizens, good neighbours, good politicians, good workmen, and good employers of labour ; the saving that limits the hours of labour, and that builds sanitary dwellings for the poor ; the saving that gives each man and woman that works, a living wage for their work, and that equalises the laws between rich and poor and puts women on an equal plane of privilege and rights with men.

What did *we* think of any of these things when we were young ? And yet the young generation now are full of them. And for my part I think they are ahead of us, and I personally mean to do all I can to help and not hinder their work. I do not believe the Christianity of Christ meant a selfish absorption in the future salvation of one's own soul, nor an introverted watching of one's internal " experiences ". I believe we were meant to " commit the keeping of our souls to Him as to a faithful Creator " and were to bend all our energies in trying to make His kingdom come on earth as it is in Heaven. And the young people of the present day *are* doing this last, whether they have consciously done the first or not. I can joyfully commit them to the Divine Master whom they are thus serving, though it may be unconsciously, and can leave it with Him to lead them by the right paths to a knowledge of Himself. Christianity to my mind does not *exclude* them that are " weak in the faith ", but rather throws its arms around them and *includes* them ; and we who profess to share the spirit of Christ must do the same.

The next matter of interest is that Ray and Karin got me up on top of a haystack ! I tell you this to show you to what lengths grandmothers 62 years old can be induced to go by their grandchildren ! We

are having splendid crops of hay off of our meadows
this year, and Robert has it all put, as is the English
custom, in great stacks. This one was covered with a
tent cloth, until there was time to thatch it with straw,
and the children used it for an aerial play-house, the
tent cloth being stretched high enough from the top to
make a delightful sort of house. We climbed up a
ladder against the side. It was great fun to the children to get grandma up there, but I confess it was a
mixed cup for me! Ray said to her mother afterwards, "Mother, I think a great deal of what an
advantage it is to us children to live near such a kind
grandma as grandma Smith. It would be so dreadful
if she was not kind." You can imagine how pleased
I was with this speech! And then she added after a
moment's thought, "I don't believe there is any other
grandma in the world who would climb up on top of
a haystack when her chickies asked her." I confess
I am rather inclined to this last opinion myself!

I seem to be hale and hearty still. But I have lots
of delightful little reminders that I am growing old,
such as rheumatic twinges, and stiff joints, and a growing sense that the burdens of this generation are no
longer on my shoulders. My dear friend, Lady Mount
Temple, feels the approach of old age to be very sad.
While I was staying with her at Torquay, we had a
visit from a most saintly Roman Catholic priest, Father
Vaughan, a brother of Cardinal Vaughan, and he
very nearly made a Catholic of her! He assured her
that all her spiritual troubles arose from the fact that
she had never been baptised, and he promised her if
she would only allow him to baptise her, all her doubts
and difficulties would vanish never to return! She was
very much tempted to try it, " like a new medicine "
I told her; and she declares that it was only my

influence that withheld her ! [1] I told him that she *had* been baptised, as an infant, in the English Church but he said he was sure it had not been rightly done and therefore was not valid, or she would not be hungering so for the water of life. I asked him what constituted a valid baptism, and he said the one vital thing was that the words " In the name of the Father, Son and Holy Ghost " should be pronounced at the identical moment when the water touched the forehead of the person being baptised ; that if there was a moment of time between the two things the baptism was not valid ; and he said that in baptisms in the English Church these fatal moments did continually intervene through carelessness or ignorance of the vital point at issue, and consequently most of their baptisms were invalid !

To her friends

Aet. 63.

PARIS, *April* 15, 1895

We find Logan's Apartment such a delightful place to stop at here. This French way of living in the Latin Quarter is so simple and so cheap, and one feels so virtuously economical, that every day is a fresh delight.

Everybody is absorbed in their studies or their work, and the whole atmosphere is one of earnest purpose and eager thought. At every turn you meet the girls walking to their studios or their Art Schools with their canvasses under their arms and a camp stool in their hands, and nobody seems to be aimless or idle. The one thing that troubles me about it is the fearful waste of enthusiasm and effort that goes on from year to year ; for of course most of all this Art studying comes to absolutely nothing. I shudder to think of the

[1] See Note I at end of Chapter.

thousands of wretched daubs that are being turned out year after year in these Paris *Ateliers* ; each one representing a whole world of enthusiasm and earnest work, and often an infinity of sacrifice on the part of parents and friends ; and all to end in hopeless failure.

It seems to me a never ending tragedy. What effect it all has upon the character and future lives of these thousands of mediocre Art Students I do not know, but I should fear that they would be utterly unfitted for any sort of quiet home life in the future. But perhaps they go out West somewhere and astonish the natives with their creations, and adorn the walls of frame farm-houses and country inns with the latest fashions in French Impressionist Art ! Let us hope that they find appreciation somewhere at last.

To Mrs. Lawrence

Aet. 63.

LONDON, *May* 12, 1895

I had a prophecy from a " Palmist " the other day, that I am to die at 67. Of course I place no faith in it, but I cannot tell thee what a real inward spring of joy it gives me every now and then to think—" Suppose it should be true ! "

To Mrs. Lawrence

Aet. 64.

LONDON, *July* 4, 1896

We have just had a regular " Opening " of Lady Henry Somerset's Inebriate Farm Home at Duxhurst by Princess Mary, the Duchess of Teck. Nothing in England is " opened " right unless it is opened by Royalty, so we were most thankful to be able to secure

the Princess Mary of Teck for ours. It is certainly
most self-sacrificing of the Royalties to do it, for drearier
or more boring functions I cannot well imagine, that
is for the Royalties. For those of us who will endure
any moment of dreariness and boredom for the sake of
catching glimpses of a Royal person, (and this I grieve
to say includes the *whole* English nation) such functions
are not so bad. I never saw one before, and I never
want to see one again. I can imagine all future ones,
without having to stand in the broiling sun for hours,
and then see nothing but a fat old lady, who looked
like any other old lady, patting some mortar on a stone
with a silver trowel !

Alas ! how little we can do at our best in bearing
one another's burdens. One finds this out more and
more as one grows older. I used to feel a capacity
for relieving everyone of their burdens in the most
successful and triumphant manner, and did not
hesitate to rush in boldly even into the most delicate
and critical affairs. But now all this desire has
vanished and I am glad, instead of interfering with
other people's burdens, to shift my own off on to
younger and stronger shoulders. I suppose this is
partly old age, and partly experience which has taught
me how easy it is to do more harm than good by interfering. But in one direction I do not believe you can
often go wrong, and that is in giving your hearty
sympathy to everybody you come in contact with. I
believe sympathy is one of the most helpful helps one
can bestow upon one's fellow creatures ; and it seems
a great pity that so many people feel it their duty to
criticise rather than sympathise.

I am sure this is where old people oftenest fail in their
relations with the young. They think that their duty to
the young requires that they should keep a sharp look-

out for their faults and mistakes, and should never fail to *reprove* them. Whereas I feel sure the contrary method is by far the most effectual, and that what we old people ought to do is to keep a sharp lookout for the virtues and the wise actions of the young, and never fail to *commend* them. It is a universal law of human nature that what we are commended for we like to repeat, and a judicious system of sympathetic appreciation is to my thinking the most effective " discipline " the world knows.

And this reminds me that I have just had published a revised edition of my little book about mothers. I say I have had it published but the fact is that Nisbets, who published the " Secret " asked permission to publish it, and of course I was nothing loth, for I like my " wise " ideas about true motherhood to be spread as widely as possible for the sake of the precious children everywhere.

I think, speaking of children, I must repeat to you the greatest compliment I ever had paid to me, that was given me by my little granddaughters the other day. We were going out in a cab together to buy some Christmas things, and one of them said, " I expect Grandma you have just got some of your income from America, so you will buy us whatever we want. " I assented to this ; and then Ray said, evidently trying to adjust this ready assent to such a sweeping system of purchase with her ideas of economy,—" I suppose you might as well use up your income while you are alive, for when you die that will be the end of it." " Oh, no," I replied, " that will not be the end. It will go on just the same, only it will be divided into 3 portions, between your Mother, and Uncle Logan, and Aunty Loo ; and then I expect your Mother will buy things for you just as I do." " Oh, no," said Ray with an air of great conviction, " she won't do it like you. Nobody *could* do things like you do ; there could not be any-body like you in all the world ! " " Why not ? " I asked. " Oh, because you are different," replied Ray, " anybody can see you are different by just looking at you." " Yes," chimed in Karin, " the corners of your mouth are always turned up in a smile ; and even your nose turns up in a smiling way." " Yes," added Ray, " and even your wrinkles have a smiling turn at their ends." Could flattery rise higher ? But I think if one can make one's *wrinkles* smile for little children, the secret of a happy old age is on the fair way to discovery.

Ray and Karin, I must say it, are little angels of goodness ; and in fact are *never* naughty unless some grown-up person makes them so. Their one greatest enjoyment in life is having me read to them stories of adventure. For a long time, Fairy stories were what they most enjoyed, but now these are second, and the wildest tales of adventure by land and sea are all they care for. Every morning I go in and sit with them while they have their breakfasts, and then I must pick out of the morning paper all the accounts of shipwrecks, and wonderful discoveries, and inventions, and impor-tant political events.

I must tell you of another speech of Ray's that does not perhaps reflect quite so much credit on me ! They were in here to tea, and I gave Karin a little reproof for some fault of table manners, when Ray said, " Now, Grandma, please don't make any moral remarks. We have plenty of morals at home, and we come in here for sprees ! "

Some of you say my pictures look too old, but I assure you I do not consider this the least of a compliment. Nothing pleases me better than to be called the " old lady " ; and when the cabmen or the navvies in the street call me " mother ", as they often do, I am delighted. I am like the Chinese, who consider it a sign of wisdom to be old, and who always say, when told the age of a visitor, " Oh, I should have thought that you were *much* older," considering this the greatest compliment they can pay. Meanwhile, however, I keep up all my old activities, and act, I am afraid, more like a young woman than an old one, in the way of work and meetings of all sorts. I have made up my mind to go on till I drop in my traces, as long as I can put one foot before the other. But I am, I admit, a little stiff with rheumatism, and sometimes find it difficult to get about. One of my troubles is that I can only lift my feet a certain height, and often, when the step of the bus or cab is a little higher than usual, I have to ask some kind passer-by to lift one foot for me, so you can imagine that it is rather awkward.

Since I last wrote we have all been greatly stirred up about the County Council Elections, which took place on March 2nd. The whole city was agitated over them for weeks, and our Temperance women were working like slaves night and day to stir up the women voters to a sense of responsibility.

To her daughter, Mary Costelloe (Berenson)
Aet. 64.

LONDON, *Oct.* 3, 1896

Mrs. Tollemache had a stroke of paralysis, and is lying unconscious ; and through it all Lady Mount Temple raves against God one minute, and does not believe there is any God the next minute. . . . I must tell thee a little piece of personal news, which need not be published, and that is that I have discarded

Pyjamas forever, and have taken to the old-fashioned nightgowns to my *great* satisfaction. I have stuffed my old Pyjamas in the Mission Bag.

To her daughter, Mary Costelloe (Berenson)
Aet. 64.

LONDON, *Oct.* 29, 1896

I am just off to Canterbury for some meetings which I promised 6 months ago. It is dreadful the way I get entangled up in meetings without meaning to. There seems to be something occult about it. Lady Henry can gaily give her engagements up when the time comes, but an uncompromising Quaker fidelity to engagements makes me stick faithfully to mine, alas !

To her daughter, Mary Costelloe (Berenson)
Aet. 64.

LONDON, *Nov.* 5, 1896

How delicious about Edith Burroughs ! But alas ! how little she knows about the prose side of having a baby. As for taking a day off for it, she is far more likely to have to take a month, and be thankful if she gets off with that. . . . I used to think babies were the one supreme thing to be desired, but I shrink from the thought of them now.

To her daughter, Alys Russell
Aet. 64.

LONDON, *Nov.* 19, 1896

This evening Miss X (of Boston) is going to dine with Lord Russell. She wanted to know if I thought it would be proper for her to dine alone with him at an hotel, especially as his Trial is on hand. I told her I was the very last person in the world to ask if anything was proper,—that I had not the least idea of the proprieties. So after a little humming and hawing she decided to go.

Later. After all Miss X did not dine with Lord Russell. After accepting, she got a letter from him to say that his Solicitor said it would not do without a chaperone. She and I do not know whether to be provoked, or amused, or mortified !

Nov. 24, 1896

Last night when we were playing whist in the drawing-room, a smell of tobacco smoke came meandering up the stairs, and I went down to blow William up. But lo and behold, I found Lord Russell in my room, writing a note to Miss X with a cigar in his mouth. He was writing an apology for putting her off from the dinner the other evening, and was asking her to another dinner tomorrow with Santayana and Marsh, but she does not mean to go.

To her daughter, Alys Russell
Aet. 64.

LONDON, *Dec.* 1, 1896

Father took a drive today in Battersea Park, but not with me. He would not let me go with him, said we were too fat to sit comfortably together in a hansom ! . . . Thee *did* stir up a commotion at Bryn Mawr ! But what an idiot that Professor Norton was ! I daresay a little of my judicious pruning would have been an advantage to thy lecture [on the Payment of Motherhood]. . . . You can say things in England that cannot be understood in America, and it is always well to keep this in mind. When I was young it was considered indecent to have a baby, and I myself was made to feel as if I was a prostitute when I had my first baby ! And I was awfully shocked when I came over to England the first time, and heard Edward Clifford talk freely and with an open face of somebody going to have a baby. It took me a long time to be convinced that he was really a decent man ! . . . How strange it is that men get so entrapped with women of a lower class than themselves. I suppose they flatter them.

To her son, Logan Pearsall Smith
Aet. 65.

PARIS, *Jan.* 1, 1897

I do not preach much, as I am sure thee will give me credit for, but I just want to say that but for my unwavering faith in a God of love and wisdom, and my absolute certainty that He cares for me and mine, I should have been crushed with despair long ago. Life has not contained much trouble for thee yet, darling son, but when it comes, remember that thy Mother has assured thee that there *is* comfort and peace in the grand fact that *God is*.

To her friends
Aet. 65.

LONDON, *April* 5, 1897

Paramount above all others has been the burning question of Greece and Crete. No doubt you are following this question with deep interest, but with you it is not a personal question ; and, after the shameful action of the U.S. Government in regard to the

Arbitration Treaty, I daresay you are not sorry to see the English Government acting in such a wicked manner towards Crete. Here it is a matter of personal concern to every man, woman and child, and we hardly think or talk of anything else. Even Ray and Karin are all stirred up about it, and ask me every morning when I go in to their breakfast, what is the last news, and whether the English ships are firing on Crete, and what Lord Salisbury has done since the day before. Nothing would do but they must send the following telegram to " Lord Salisbury, Foreign Office—We beg you not to let the English Fleet coerce Greece. Ray and Karin, two little girls." We are all wearing little buttons with the Greek flag on, and we are holding meetings and Demonstrations without number. And meanwhile the Government, through the mouth of Mr. George Curzon, sneers and jokes, and prevaricates, and the accursed work of upholding the great Assassin goes calmly on.

I confess my Quaker testimony against war has become very unstable of late. There seems no way in which this matter *can* be settled but by a war that will exterminate Turkey ; and I wish from the bottom of my heart that America would step in and support the Greeks, and give the wicked " Concert of Europe " an object lesson in what a free nation is willing to do to help another nation to be free ! I can assure you that I have actually wished I was a man and young enough to go over to Greece to help them fight ; and I almost wondered at some of the meetings, where I have been stirred to the very depths, that I did not come out with a helmet on my head ! I never had the slightest idea before of what an overpowering enthusiasm for freedom is like, and I do not wonder now that people have died to secure it.

To her friends

Aet. 65.

FRIDAY'S HILL, *Aug.* 4, 1897

Just now the children are occupied in building a grand Fort in a tree at the bottom of our meadows, and the sound of their voices comes up over the green grass, through the open windows as I sit and write, filling my old grandmotherly heart with happy content.

We have quite a little colony around us this summer, and generally have a crowd of young and old daily to tea. As they all belong to the younger generation Robert and I sit placidly on one side and listen to their " clash-ma-clavers " with the indulgent tolerance of old age, and chuckling inwardly to think that some day they in their turn will have to listen to the clash-ma-clavers of the generation after them with the same indulgence. I cannot say that we *agree* with all they say but I am thoroughly convinced that each generation, whether we like it or not, is bound to have its own way of looking at things and its own problems and ways of working them out, and it is folly for the older generation to think they can make the young ways conform to the old ones. But the younger generation around us are all so good and right-minded that I do not feel any anxiety ; and as I know that God loves them as He does us, and cares for them as tenderly, I feel sure He will lead them by the right way into His fold, perhaps by the *South* gate, while our entrance was by the *North* gate, but none the less safely into its green pastures and beside its still waters.

L

To her friends

Aet. 65.

VENICE, *Nov.* 4, 1897

On November 1st and 2nd it was the feasts of " All Saints " and " All Souls ", and the whole population of Venice seemed to flock over to the island of San Michele, which is occupied with the Cemetery of Venice, to adorn the graves of their friends with wreaths and flowers and candles, and to weep over them. We got into our gondola on the afternoon of the 2nd and joined in the long procession of gondolas that was taking the crowd across the Lagoon for this yearly function. It was a most picturesque and interesting occasion.

The whole island is enclosed as a Cemetery, and the graves are all in rows, marked mostly by a tiny stone with the name on, but sometimes by an iron cross bearing elaborate wreaths of flowers or beads. Little groups were gathered about the graves here and there, arranging the flowers or placing the candles among the grass, and then saying a few prayers, and cheerfully hurrying away to join the strollers over the grass, and to have some congenial gossip about their living friends, who were evidently much more interesting to them than their dead ones. Among all the groups I only saw one where any tears were shed, and even they were soon done with. It was a vivid commentary to me on the fact that when we go out of this life, our places are quickly filled up, and our friends are speedily consoled. And of course this is as it should be, for the blessed Gospel of Christ teaches us that to depart and be with the Lord is such a boon that only selfishness can mourn over it when it comes to those we love.

To Miss Olive Seward

Aet. 66.

LONDON, *Mar.* 28, 1898

What a wonderful ovation at Miss Willard's death ! It has been more than even I expected, and yet I have always known she was greatly beloved. Personally the loss to myself is simply irreparable. But I do not mourn. I think rather of what it must be to her to have got to the blessed peace where all secrets are revealed, and where, every hindrance being removed, her spirit can break forth into its fullest development. My sympathy in her delight will not suffer me to think of *my* side of it. And then too I shall so soon join her ! At least I hope so, for it seems to me one of the greatest of boons to be allowed to say farewell to this earth life while one is in the midst of one's activities, rather than linger on to be a cumberer of the ground and a burden to oneself and to all around. God chose the right moment for Frances, and I am glad. I would not have detained her for a single hour.

My two little grandchildren are great darlings, and make us very happy. They are devout little Catholics, and seem to enjoy their religion, and I am glad of it. I daresay they will be saved a good many of the perplexities and difficulties that so often beset Protestant children.

I belong to a Committee called " The Friends of Armenia ", and I am appalled at the condition of things. It appears that as soon as the Armenians begin to be a little prosperous, the tax gatherers swoop down upon them and rob them of all their earnings. It is altogether a most difficult and perplexing question. There almost seems some occult power at work against the Armenians, for everything connected with them seems invariably to get into some sort of a snarl. Armenian Committees seem nearly always to quarrel, Armenian Homes end in failure, Armenian workers become disgusted and throw it all up, and nothing connected with the subject seems to prosper. I do not understand it.

To her daughter, Alys Russell

Aet. 67.

LONDON, *Feb.* 23, 1899

I saw Canon Wilberforce open Parliament yesterday, and then stayed up in the Cage, and heard John Morley's speech, which was very anti-Jingo. I expect just the kind of talk as is going on in the United States Senate at the present time. *He* was against extending the Empire by taking in the Soudan, and *theirs* is against taking in the Philippines, but both using the same arguments. I wanted to shout down out of the Cage, " It is the destiny of the Anglo-Saxon race— their mission to the World ! " But John Morley would have pooh-poohed at such stuff as that. I had to content myself with unloosing a screw in that uncivilised " Cage ", and bringing it away as *my* contribution towards the civilising of England itself !

May 21

Aunt Margaret and I were not at all pleased with " La Belle Otero ". She was not particularly handsome, and her dancing was a whirl of legs and skirts that to my thinking was really ugly. We are *done* with Music Halls !

To her friends

Aet. 67.

FRIDAY'S HILL, *July* 31, 1899

We have been busy with the unexpected By
Election [1] in East St. Pancras, for which Mr. Costelloe
was the Liberal Candidate, and Alys and I had to
work for him.   The first evening of the campaign the
Chairman introduced me as the mother-in-law of the
Candidate, and said when a man's mother-in-law
vouched for him no one could doubt his worthiness.
So when I got up to speak, I began with, " Yes, I am
his mother-in-law ", and the whole audience roared
and cheered in the wildest kind of way.   After the
meeting, a crowd collected around the door as I came
out and shouted, " Well, mother-in-law !   Hurrah,
mother-in-law !   We'll put him in, Mother-in-law ! "
etc. etc.

And all through the campaign (which fortunately
lasted only ten days) whenever I appeared in the
constituency I was greeted everywhere with cries of
" Hey, mother-in-law !   There she is !   Hurrah for
mother-in-law ! "   And the women all pointed and
grinned, and held up their babies for me to see.   The
day of the Election we had a Coach and Four with
red-coated outriders blowing their horns, and several
landaus following, all covered with placards, " Vote
for Costelloe, The People's Friend ", and the occupants
wearing red favours, which were his colours, and I
carrying a red parasol.

[1] For the London County Council.

To her friends

Aet. 67.

AIX-LES-BAINS, *Aug.* 26, 1899

To my unqualified amazement, on August 19th I was whisked off here to take the " Cure " for my stiffness. I consented to come on one condition, namely, that, if this fails to help me, I shall hereafter be left in peace to stiffen up at my own good pleasure.

Of course we have all heard of the " gay and wicked world " that congregated at Aix, and I expected to be shocked and horrified at every step. But I confess thus far my expectations have been disappointed. Aix seems to be taken possession of by fat, rheumatic, lame, middle-aged Matrons,—French, German, English and Americans, and wherever we go these are the people we meet.

We even went to the " Casino ", where we supposed the " gay and wicked world " would certainly congregate, but even there the same limping, frumpy but eminently respectable procession passed before us, each rheumatic mother attended by a daughter who seemed to be a pattern of filial piety. Perhaps our eyes are too pure to behold iniquity, or else we have not yet found out where to look, for certain it is as yet no " gay and wicked world " has come within our ken. Mary, however, who is taking French lessons, says her French teacher tells her that the " Demi-Monde " have taken possession of the Hotels down in the Town, and that all the respectable visitors are obliged to go to the Hotels up the sides of the mountains, where we are.

There was to be a " Battle of Flowers " one day, and my niece Carey Thomas and her friend Mary Garrett took Mary and myself in their landau adorned with great bunches of Gladiolus tied on each lamp, and with a basket of fifty small bouquets all ready to join in the " Battle ". I had read so many accounts of these Battles of Flowers, describing them as being so transcendently beautiful and bewitching, that I confess I expected great things. But it turned out to be a most second-rate sort of an affair, with a few carriages rather prettily trimmed with flowers, and a good many, like our own, with only enough flowers to make them presentable.

We went round and round a large field in a procession, throwing our little bouquets of flowers at the people in the stands, and being pelted by them in return, and it seemed to us the silliest sort of child's play. An old friend of mine used to say that it was always a gain when one found out what one did not want to do, and I certainly found out that day that I did not want to go to any more " Batailles des Fleurs ". I wondered whether it could be possible that the Papers would give the same enthusiastic description of this stupid affair as I had seen of other " Batailles ", and sure enough, you might have supposed from their enthusiastic reports that it had been one of the most beautiful and bewitching functions. So I conclude the other descriptions that so beguiled me, must have been equally misleading.

Sept. 10. After writing the above, we had a glimpse of the " gay and wicked world " after all.

We went one evening to the " Cercle ", I felt it necessary to dress up to the part, so I put on a bonnet of Mary's with red velvet trimmings and looked quite " gay " ! and there we saw enough to convince us that there was in very truth a gay and wicked world in Aix. The gaming tables were crowded, and were a sickening spectacle, and gaily dressed women thronged

through the Halls and Gardens.   Except the gambling
we saw nothing especially wicked, but we saw the
possibilities of it, and were convinced by ocular proof
that there were other people besides rheumatic fat old
matrons congregating in Aix.

To her friends

Aet. 69.

LONDON, *Feb.* 18, 1901

There is one thing which the death of my son-in-
law, Frank Costelloe, has accomplished and which I do
not believe anything else could, and that is it has made
me WANT TO LIVE ! I feel as if I should be really
needed for 9 or 10 more years, in order to make an
English home for my grandchildren and to avoid the
complications that would inevitably arise in regard
to their guardianship if I should die. As it is I
am appointed by the Court of Chancery the *acting
Guardian*,[1] and the custody of the children is given to
me, and for their sakes I feel it is important for me to
live until they are of age.   So I have put on one side
my eager desire to " depart and be with Christ " and
am content to defer the joys of the other life until I
am not needed any longer to protect my precious
grandchildren here.

I confess it feels very funny to want to live, after
having for so long looked forward with such an eager
desire to go.   However, so it is, and I give you liberty

[1] When Costelloe died, his wife having left him, he set down in his
will that the two daughters should be brought up, on the small income
he had bequeathed them, by a Roman Catholic lady.   H.W.S. managed
to get the two girls appointed wards in chancery, to be brought up under
her care, in her more comfortable and affluent home.   She covenanted
that they should be educated as Roman Catholics, and she kept, as her
letters reveal, strictly to her promise.

to wish me many happy returns of my future birthdays, or rather I should say *10* happy returns, for in 10 years both Ray and Karin will be of age, and will be free from the Chancery Court, and from all danger of interference by any opposing guardian. If you had only known this when you wrote me those lovely letters on my 69th birthday, you might have freely wished me these 10 happy returns. It was a great joy to me to receive your letters. Most of them arrived on the very birthday itself. I had been away from home for two or three days attending some of our Temperance meetings in Boston, Lincs., and got home on my birthday, and in the evening came all your delightful letters, to my great surprise, for I had actually forgotten myself that it was my birthday, and had never dreamed that anyone else would remember it.

I wish you could all have been here to see me open one letter after another, and hear my exclamations of delight and surprise as each fresh loving message revealed itself. Of course I knew well enough that I was not half as good and nice as you made out, but then I am awfully glad you think I am, and it spurred me up to try and come up to your estimate of me more and more.

If you will not think it *too* egotistical I will quote an extract from the Boston papers showing what some people thought of me there. " Mrs. Pearsall Smith was the shining light among the speakers, for a more charming, amusing and at the same time sweet old lady has rarely been heard in Boston." I shall put all your letters away in an envelope marked " Letters on my 69th birthday ", so that my future descendants may know, if they come across them, what dear and kind friends their old ancestor had !

Not long ago I was speaking at a meeting on this question of children going to the Public Houses, and when I sat down, a Clergyman got up and said, " Why I never knew that children did go, and I think the speaker must be mistaken." And he was a bald-headed clergyman too, and must have lived in the world several years. Why the fact is that you never see a Public House anywhere without seeing a child, either going in or coming out, with a jug or a can of liquor, and very often tasting it as they go along.

Not to be outdone by the younger generation, I too am preparing something for publication. It is a part of my autobiography, and I call it " How I discovered God ". It is the story of my soul life from my early Quaker days, on through all the progressive steps of my experience until I reach that peace which cannot fail to come to the soul who has " discovered God " ! —I am putting all my heresies into my story, and am trying to show the steps that have led to them ; and I flatter myself that it is going to be very convincing ! So if you feel afraid of becoming heretics, I advise you not to read it. For my part, I always *did* love being a heretic as some of you know. What fun it was in those old days when our little flock of " Mystic Birds " used to be taking our mystic flights higher and higher into the unexplored regions of God's love, and how restful it is now, in our old age, to have folded our wings in the blessed haven of absolute certainty that *God is enough !* All religion is enfolded for me now in these three words. God is enough for me, and for everybody, and for all the needs of all the limitless universe He has created !

To her daughter, Mary Berenson
Aet. 69.

LONDON, *Sept.* 8, 1901

Karin and Ray made up this poem while they were dressing this morning, and came dancing downstairs exclaiming, " Oh, grandma, we have made up *such* a wicked song about the Prefects at school ! It is dreadfully wicked. If they were to hear of it at school, we would be expelled." What dear innocent wickedness it is !

To her daughter, Mary Berenson
Aet. 69.

LONDON, *Oct.* 26, 1901

The children pity thee profoundly for being bored, and say, now thee knows how *they* feel when the stupid old people are around and they have to sit still and listen.

It almost makes me sick not to pay my bills when they are due.

Lady Mount Temple's death-bed was a scene of strife—Juliet kept lighting candles, and one of the dear Lady's nieces kept blowing them out. Then Juliet kept trying to moisten the Lady's parched lips, and " Uncle Augustus " kept snatching the sponge from her and saying no one should touch his sister but himself. I believe, however, that Juliet conquered in both cases. I tell Alys I shall engage a policeman to be present at my death-bed, so that if Ray lights candles and Alys blows them out, he may interfere to preserve order.

Nov. 28, 1901

I spoke last evening to a congregation of the *very* ugliest people I ever laid eyes on. They sang " We are marching to Heaven ", and it seemed impossible such ugly beings could ever get any entrance there ; and then I had a Quaker " opening " on the absolute independence of the soul from the body, and I saw behind a face that was the double distilled essence of ugliness, a really beautiful soul, and could actually have kissed her !

What a regular free Pension you keep for out-of-elbow people ! I should hate it. Thee is like thy father. I used to say of him that he stood at the corner of the street, and rang a bell to call in every disreputable religious tramp that was within hearing. Yours are hardly religious, but artistic tramps are as bad. And the way *we* were imposed on was something awful.

Nov. 26, 1901

The whole secret of comfort in cold weather is very simple—to put on two or even three complete suits of underclothes, two pairs of woollen stockings, warm woollen gloves (not kid), warm coats, a warm rug or even two, and a foot warmer. Also have a knit shawl to wrap around thy head. With this armour, I do not think the cold on the journey will be at all formidable. Have a hot bottle, that can be filled at the stopping places, to hold in thy lap or to put at thy feet.

Feb. 16, 1902

Thy letter about Carlyle and Emerson interests me very much. It shows that after all your " top eyes " are not entirely closed, and your spirits are not altogether earthbound. I often and often wonder how it is that people so fundamentally good as you are can be so content without any real link with God, and even, I fear, without any certainty that there is a God to be linked to. My soul was always so full of aspirations, that a God was a necessity to me. I was like a bird with an instinct of migration upon me, and a country to migrate to was as essential as it is to the bird. But you have seemed content to sit on a branch and merely flap the wings that were meant for flying, and to let your horizon be bounded by the fences of one little field, with no longings for the great spaces of the eternities.

But thy letter gives a glimpse into other and higher needs of your natures, and I am delighted to see that you *would* like to fly, if you knew where the beautiful islands lie for which your spirits long. I feel hopeful somehow that the cocoons will at last open and let out the imprisoned butterfly. Religion has been to me the most " fascinating background ", as thee expresses it, to all my life. Without it, everything would have been dull and uninteresting in the extreme. I can only trust that you may come sooner or later to know its fascinations ! I remember well when Carlyle did for me just what thee describes, and I revelled in it, but religion did it even more deeply and vividly. I have tried to show this in my autobiography, but words seem rather powerless to express spiritual realities.

Even in my extreme evangelical days, what I got at was the *fact* of God's forgiveness, although I hung it on a hook that I had afterwards to discard. And all through, the one thing I was really finding out was that the Creator was doing His work of creation in an adequate and satisfactory way, and was going to make a good job of it in the end. The various hooks upon which I hung this fact at the different stages of my progress was entirely immaterial after all. The bottom fact is the only thing. And I fully believe that this bottom fact of a *good* Creator, can be got at through all sorts of religious beliefs and all sorts of religious ceremonies, and that it does not matter what these are, provided the soul is honest in regard to them.

Mar. 6, 1902

I am a little better, but the nasty influenza still hangs on, and makes me feel like the dregs of creation. It has left me with a cough that digs the very insides out of me. I shall certainly after this have more sympathy for the rest of you when you have colds. But sickness is a perfect nuisance. I feel tempted to be provoked with everybody who is sick, myself included.

Yes, there *are* dreadful possibilities all around us, but generally I think life goes on pretty quietly, and especially if we learn how to take it quietly. Somehow even tragedies seem less tragical, when you are the actors in them, than they look to outsiders.

Mar. 17, 1902

Thee may tell Aunt Janet from me that she might as well try to stop the stars in their courses as to try to stop a love affair.

To her friends

Aet. 70.

LONDON, *April* 7, 1902

I have employed a good deal of the last two months in having an attack of Influenza, and I can truly say I have not been so ill for years and years. Of course most of my public work has had to be stopped, but this has delighted me, as my lameness makes it very difficult for me to undertake meetings ; and moreover I am 70 years old, and it has long been a principle of mine that when people have arrived at the Bible limit of three score years and ten, they ought to retire altogether from active life, and give the next generation a *perfectly free field*. In my opinion one of the greatest hindrances to each generation is the undue influence and interference of the old people of the previous generation ; and I am fully determined not to be one of these hindrances. So I look at the blank spaces in my engagement book with a delightful sense of duty fulfilled, and with a most comfortable approving conscience.

To her daughter, Mary Berenson
Aet. 70.

LONDON, *April* 11, 1902

Beg the doctor to tell the exact truth and to say just what B. B.[1] ought to do for his health. I do not suppose he will do it. Nobody in the process of breaking down ever does do what they ought. But it does seem a pity. Only beg him, instead of walking, to lie out under your cypress trees and simply rest. But why do I waste my breath, for *of course* he won't do it. But my convictions are so strong that I must write it.

Why don't you let those ignorant Americans enjoy their bogus pictures in peace ? It will be all the same in a few years, and it spreads the enjoyment of the " Old Masters " over so much wider an area ! If you confine the Old Masters to the few genuine ones, what *are* most of the Americans to admire ? I believe in generosity !

[1] Mr. Bernard Berenson.

May 3, 1902

The true secret of giving advice is, after you have honestly given it, to be perfectly indifferent whether it is taken or not, and never persist in trying to set people right. That has been my secret, and I have never had any quarrels.

What if people *are* fools or knaves, it is not your housekeeping and you had far better leave them to their fate. The more you try to prove yourselves in the right and D. in the wrong, the more you will confirm him in his own views. Nothing makes people more furious than being proved to be in the wrong ; and even if you convince D. he will always hate you.

July 29, 1902

Aunt Margaret and I are very dissipated—we are going to " Caste " this afternoon, and have tickets for two things next week. Aunt Margaret never goes in Birmingham, so I am glad to give her the pleasure here. In fact, she never goes out of the house there, but here we are on the go all day long. There is the cab and we old sinners must be off.

Later. Aunt Margaret and I did not care for " Caste " this afternoon. There was too much what I call " horse-play ". We are dainty old ladies, for all we are so gay !

We have been to a Prayer Meeting for the King this afternoon, but it was a dreadfully cut-and-dried affair —no real feeling appropriate to the crisis at all. I saw tremendous possibilities if only there had been a magnetic leader who realised the real esoteric voice of the occasion. I almost felt as if I could have done it myself ! ! Instead I took furtive naps between the droning speeches and prayers. But it was an occasion of a thousand, for Queen's Hall was packed, and there was an overflow meeting, and all hearts were ready to respond to any voice of real conviction.

Logan will meet thee at Oxford, as he wants to take his MS [1] to the University Press there. What a literary family we are ! And what fun it is.

To her daughter, Alys Russell

Aet. 70.

FRIDAY'S HILL, *Aug.* 25, 1902

We are expecting Roger Fry tonight, and the Vicar is coming to dinner. So Logan and Mariechen [2] are to be told off to entertain the Vicar while Roger Fry is taken off by Berenson to Bertie Russell's Study. The Vicar confided to Grace that he was going to try and convert all the Friday's Hill household !

NOTE I (p. 127)

H.W.S. would often take successfully a matter-of-fact line with those who were troubled in their religion. In her most famous book, *The Christian's Secret of a Happy Life*, she suggests a plan for dealing with the sin of doubt, which she curiously likens to another sin : " I believe myself the only effective remedy is to take a pledge against it, as you would urge a drunkard to do against drink " ; and, later in the same chapter, she proposes a formal declaration against doubt : " If you cannot do this by word of mouth, write it in a letter . . . take up your pen and write out your determination never to doubt again."

This odd device was more effective than might be supposed ; Logan Pearsall Smith used to tell of a way she followed with a Roman Catholic lady, a convert who was vexed by doubts about some dogma of the Church—the Real Presence, I think it was. H.W.S. wrote out on a piece of paper, " I undertake never to have any more doubts about the Real Presence " (or whatever it was), and brought it to her, and made her sign it. After that the troubled spirit was utterly at rest.

---

[1] This was probably the MS. which he had discovered at Burley on the Hill, and which contained table-talk of Sir Henry Wotton's, and some unpublished letters by Donne.

[2] Mary Berenson ; the name was originally given to her by a German nurse.

X

GROWING OLD GRACEFULLY

To her daughter, Mary Berenson

Aet. 70.

LONDON, *Nov.* 25, 1902

I remember grandpa Whitall used to say, " Short visits make long friends," and I believe he was right in most cases. I have always found that long visits seemed to exhaust my powers of affection. Not of course in the case of relatives who are congenial, but of outside friends, let them be ever so congenial. There *is* something in blood that helps you to put up with things.

Nov. 28, 1902

I do hope thee won't take those feckless T.s on thy shoulders. Thee will have to learn to be content to see people make muddles of their lives in their own way. My experience has taught me that you cannot *play Providence* successfully, outside of your own family. Thy letters about X have been a *most* valuable education to the children, and I do not believe they will ever forget the lessons they have taught. It is a capital plan to teach children from the faults of other people, as it is entirely impersonal, and instead of arousing anger, it arouses a spirit of emulation.

Dec. 15, 1902

Alas ! we cannot find any key for thy unfortunate trunk ! I expect thee has it. *Why* did not one of us

think of it sooner ?   If all the bother caused by trunk
keys since the world began could be brought together
and piled up in a heap, I believe it would make a
pyramid that would reach the clouds.   And we none
of us ever learn how to take care of them, and have
them on hand when they are wanted ! !   What real
idiots we are at bottom, beneath all our Art culture
and our religious attainments !

Dec. 31, 1902

We are greatly enjoying a rich scandal about Mrs.
X's servants, who appear to have been having high
jinks while she and her husband were away.   The
great question is whether we shall tell her or not.
Prudence says not, for of course she won't believe it,
but the pleasure of " telling tales ", hidden under a
mask of duty, says " Tell ", so I do not know which
will conquer.

July 19, 1903

Has thee got my small box I loaned thee ? . . .
Never was a woman of 71 worse off for trunks than I
am, thanks to the depredations of my children.

To her daughter, Alys Russell

Aet. 70.

LONDON, *Jan.* 24, 1903

P.[1] was here last evening.   He has seen some very
striking spirit materialisations, when the spirits walked
about and talked with one another.   He was entirely

---

[1] A spiritualist named Podmore.

convinced, and firmly believes that Cardinal Newman and Napoleon appeared to him ! He said it convinced him of the reality of another world, and I told him, then he had better hurry and get ready for it.

Logan is getting ready to go. On account of Rose's [the housemaid's] absence I have not been able to see about his underclothes, etc., as she always looked them over and told me what was lacking. So I think thee had better see if he does not need stockings at least. But do not tell him I asked thee to look. Men are Kittle-Kattle at their best. Kate [the parlourmaid] is still in bed. Rose is still away. Mrs. Rollings [the maid] is still utterly disabled. Mrs. Tomlin [the charwoman] is still dead. And yet the work has still to be done !

I feel as if I should almost make a feast to celebrate Rose's return. What saints our servants are to wait on us as they do ! We never know how valuable they are to us until we can't get any. They have seemed to me lately the very hub of the universe ! If God's servants are as valuable to Him as mine are to me, we may begin to think a good deal of ourselves !

To her friends

Aet. 70.

LONDON, *Jan.* 31, 1903

We are in 1903 and I am nearly 71 years old. I always thought I should love to grow old, and I find it is even more delightful than I thought. It is so delicious to be *done* with things, and to feel no need any longer to concern myself much about earthly affairs. I seem on the verge of a most delightful journey to a place of unknown joys and pleasures, and things here seem of so little importance, compared to things there, that they have lost most of their interest for me.

I cannot describe the sort of done-with-the-world feeling I have. It is not that I feel as if I was going to die at all, but simply that the world seems to me nothing but a passage way to the real life beyond ; and passage ways are very unimportant places. It is of very little account what sort of things they contain, or how they are furnished. One just hurries through them to get to the places beyond.

My wants seem to be gradually narrowing down, my *personal* wants, I mean, and I often think I could be quite content in the Poor-house ! I do not know whether this is piety or old age, or a little of each mixed together, but honestly the world and our life in it does seem of too little account to be worth making the least fuss over, when one has such a magnificent prospect close at hand ahead of one ; and I am tremendously content to let one activity after another go, and to await quietly and happily the opening of the door at the end of the passage way, that will let me in to my real abiding place. So you may think of me as happy and contented, surrounded with unnumbered blessings, and delighted to be 71 years old.

To her daughter, Mary Berenson

Aet. 71.

LONDON, *Feb.* 22, 1903

I have just come in from an enormous meeting of poor " Mothers ". It was pitiful to see such an accumulation of trouble as my mind's eye saw behind all their stolid, stupid, care-worn faces.

Last evening the children were lamenting that Lent was so near, and I said, " Well now you must tell me what you like to have to eat instead of meat." " Oh, Grandma," exclaimed Ray, " that is not the way. Lent is meant to teach us self-denial, and you must not hunt up nice things." (All the same I shall ! But I confess it *is* a bother, which bother, I suppose, is *my* Lent.)

I am thinking of you to-day as free at last from your champion Bore. I suppose none of you have been philanthropic enough to tell her what an awful Bore she is. It seems a shame to let a human being go on like that, but I do not suppose it would have done the least good. She has served one purpose, however, and that is she has been the text for some powerful lessons to Ray and Karin on the subject of becoming Bores.

If Ray can learn to play games now without losing her temper, she will know how later to play the game of life ditto. She and Karin have decided to give up all birthday treats and presents this year for the sake of giving the money to Father Brown for a pair of candles for his new church. I thought the gift ought to involve a little self-denial on their part, and they seem quite willing. But imagine Grandpa Whitall's great-grandchildren laying up treasure in Heaven by giving candlesticks to a Roman Catholic High Altar ! I wonder if their great-grandchildren will be tearing down High Altars and breaking candlesticks.

I find I simply *cannot* go about, except just in the house, and into Rollings' old four-wheeler for my daily outing. My sprees are really over at last. My next spree will be Heaven, and that *will* be a spree worth having !

To her friends

Aet. 71.

LONDON, *May* 25, 1903

I must tell you of a funny experience I have had since I last wrote you, and which is not ended yet. With a great deal of apparent mystery a lady whom I did not know asked if she might call on me, stating that she had read my books and thought I could help her, and said she would like to bring a little invalid daughter. Of course, I arranged a time, and they came. The daughter was blind, and deformed, and only just able to walk on two crutches, but with a sweet intelligent face.

I supposed, of course, they had come for spiritual help for the poor cripple, so after a few preliminary remarks about the weather, etc., in order to make things easy, I began speaking about her trials and said that I hoped she had the comfort of saying " Thy will be done " about it all. She said very shortly " Yes ", but looked utterly uninterested and I felt quite non-plussed. An awkward pause followed, and I was wondering what I *should* say next, when the Mother said, " We came to see you, Mrs. Smith, about a very strange matter. We have an Arabian Prince living with us, and we want you to find him a wife." " A wife," I said aghast, " why how on earth am I to do that, and why do you come to me ? " " We thought," said the Mother, " that you were such a good Christian woman, and that you knew so many people, that when you heard the story you would be sure to be able to help us." And she then proceeded to unfold the story.

It seems that a wealthy Arabian Sheik, a Mahommedan, of course, conceived the desire to have his son brought up as an English gentleman, and gave him as a little boy into the care of an English lady, the sister of an explorer he had met, with a large income to support and educate the boy. Before the boy was of age the father died, and a powerful relative usurped the Sheikship, and brought influence to bear to induce the true heir to remain in England, granting him a large income, and letting him do what he pleased. Up to the age of 40, he lived a luxurious and dissipated life, and then, for some reason I could not discover, the family wanted him to come back to Arabia and to marry a Mahommedan cousin, and take possession of his property over there. But meanwhile he has become so thoroughly English that he does not want to go back, and moreover he declares he has become a Christian and *could not* be a Mahommedan again. In order to force him to accede to their wishes, his family have stopped his allowance, and he is left penniless and starving. This lady took him in as an act of Christian charity, feeling sure the family would soon give way, and the Prince, as she calls him, would repay. But time passes and nothing is done, and she begins to fear she is to be permanently saddled with him. Finally the family have sent over an emissary to say that if the Prince will give up his wandering life and will marry an upper class English woman, one who has never done anything to earn her own living, and will settle down as an English gentleman, they will then restore him his income, and will settle the sum of £25,000 on his wife; and it is this wife I am asked to find !

The Prince's name is Hafiz Abicedes. No question of *love* seems to enter into the proceedings ; all he asks is for a woman who is a lady, and who has never worked for her living. It is no matter how poor she may be, provided this taint of earning money by her work has never touched her. So you see I am asked to be a Matrimonial Agent in a private way ! Perhaps somebody who reads this letter may feel inclined to become a Princess, and to secure the dower of £25,000, and let the Prince be thrown in as part of the bargain ! Needless to say, no wife has fallen to the bait yet, and I do not know where to find one.

The one matter of public interest that is absorbing all thoughts just now is the new Education Bill. Personally I cannot join the Passive Resisters because I seem to see both sides of the question, which is a thing that often happens in old age, and although I consider the Bill most unfair and in fact on some accounts really iniquitous, I shall still go on paying my taxes, until I get a stronger conviction as to what is right to do.

The next thing proposed, and this was something in which I could heartily join, was a great Hyde Park Demonstration. I thought, however, that I was too lame to think of accompanying it, but when the day came, May 23rd, the impulse was so strong that I determined to make an effort, and by dint of being pushed and pulled by my kind friends, I found myself seated in a high brake, and I thoroughly enjoyed it. It was a grand Demonstration, at least 100,000 people : and a tremendous body of conscientious conviction. I do not suppose, however, that anything will come of it. To Balfour (if he hears of it at all, which I doubt) it will seem nothing more than a demonstration of poodle dogs, and it will not affect him in the slightest. It is hopeless to try and fight against people who do not know that you exist.

When the Resolution condemning the Bill had been put there was a moment's hush, and then a deafening emphatic "Aye! Aye!" thundered out from a 100,000 throats in a simultaneous roar of applause and approval. It almost seemed as if Balfour on his golf links must have heard it and trembled!

I have sent in my resignation as the Secretary of the British Women's Temperance Association. I told them last year I intended to do so on account of my age, as it is a fixed principle with me that after people are 70 they have no right to continue occupying official positions, but are in duty bound to step out and leave room for the next generation. I might have found it hard to carry out my purpose in face of the urgent entreaties I have had to continue at least a year longer in office ; but Providence has stepped in to my rescue by letting my lameness become so much worse during the past year that now it is almost a matter of physical impossibility for me to get about to the meetings, and this, if nothing else, would force me to resign.

I look upon my lameness therefore as a mark of the Divine approval of my intended laying aside of the duties I have so long tried faithfully to perform. I have loved the work, and have loved the women, and I think they have loved me, and we have been very happy together. Of course I shall still keep up my interest in the Association and shall do what I can to help, but my day for meetings is pretty much over. If I stand up to speak, I seem to turn into a stone image, and find it almost impossible to bend enough to sit down again. And the exertion of getting up the stairs to a meeting or even on to the platform is really more than I am equal to. I was able, as I have told you, to make a tremendous spurt, and be pushed and pulled up into the Brake for the Hyde Park Demonstration, but one cannot go through such pushing and pulling operations in meetings before congregations, and this week's meetings are my last. Otherwise I feel very well and very happy, and in many ways quite as young as ever, so I am well content.

To her son, Logan Pearsall Smith
Aet. 71.

LONDON, *May* 28, 1903

I took my leave of the British Women's Temperance Association to-day, and they gave me an Illuminated Address—a most flattering one—(I would not let them give anything else) and speeches were made equally flattering, and I responded flattering them, and we had a universal flattering time, and everyone was happy, and not a tear was shed. I have had a delightful time in the work, and now I shall have a delightful time out of it.

To her daughter, Mary Berenson
Aet. 71.

LONDON, *July* 7, 1903

I am just off now with the youngsters and Grace to see " In Dahomey "—a Play with real Darkies and a real Cake Walk. But Madam Ray refuses to go, for she says she knows it will be vulgar, and *she* doesn't like vulgar things ! Grace and I feel quite sat upon, but we love Darkies, in their proper place, and mean to enjoy it.

Ray heard, as usual, a long dissertation about Westminster School from Val, who seems to have no other idea in his head. I asked Ray if she had had a chance to bring in anything about Kensington School, but she said he would not listen to a word. I tell her that is the way with men, and that if you want to get at their hearts, you must let them talk about themselves and their interests, and say nothing about your own interests.

It makes me perfectly indignant to have the girls forced to keep on at school during all this hot weather. If I were only younger, I would make such a stir that for peace sake the High School Council would have to change it. But my time for reforming the world has passed, although I have just done something that I do not dare to tell anyone about for a while yet.

To her daughter, Mary Berenson

Aet. 71.

LONDON, *July* 9, 1903

What I have been " up to " is this. At Westminster School there is a system by which big boys are not only allowed but encouraged to beat the younger boys, just as they please, without the intervention of any of the Masters ; and as a consequence, it is done for every little trivial pretext, and often most unjustly, and sometimes very brutally. It simply makes me *furious* ! I know what boys of 17 and 18 are, and to put into their hands such irresponsible power seems to me a sure and certain education in brutality.

Finally I got so worked up about it that I wrote a severe letter to Dr. Gow, the Head Master, telling him just what I thought, and asserting that such a system was the direct cause of " ragging " in the British Army, and ending with a threat that unless some change was made, the matter would have to be aired in the Public Press. I wrote anonymously as an " old inhabitant of Westminster ", and had the letter typewritten. Thee must not speak of it, as it would get Val into trouble if it was known to be me. I *hope* it gave old Gow a bad quarter of an hour.

I shall follow it up with another letter, if the thing goes on. It is an outrage on civilisation. My old " mush spoon " still has life in it !

To her daughter, Mary Berenson

Aet. 71.

LONDON, *Dec.* 27, 1903

Well, the children all got off to the country this morning, but it *was* a work. Owing to the fact of the three holidays, Friday, Saturday and Sunday, no supplies could be purchased either in London or at Haslemere, so I had to go off before breakfast in Rollings to get them vegetables and meat. They were going down at 11.15, so there was no time to spare. I also had to get eggs, as Mrs. Venes wrote me that none could be got down there for love or money, and also cake for their teas. However, everything was got and packed, and they caught their train, and then at 11 o'clock I had my breakfast in peace, with a well-earned appetite.

Jan. 2, 1904

No word of any sort from the wretches ! But they are too full of their fun to have time for letters. I have noticed that letters are generally the outcome of being bored by everything else, so I always think, no letters, no boredom.

To her daughter, Mary Berenson

Aet. 71.

LONDON, *Jan.* 21, 1904

Ellie confided to her aunt that when the girls were alone in the country they got up at 3 o'clock in the morning and went out for a walk in the woods ! Ray had not told me that ! Perhaps if they are allowed to do it unmolested two or three times, they will get enough of it, as they have of camping out. It is generally the forbidden thing that human nature enjoys most. *Why* is this ?

There was hockey this afternoon, although the ground is still muddy. Then at 6 came the " Religious Instructor ", and the children begged me to be sure to go. Thee may imagine that I banged it for all I was worth !

To-day I ventured to say to Ray, not that she was growing older, oh no, but only that she was less childish than she used to be ; but she would not listen to me for a moment, and declared that if we said such things, she would go right back and be a baby again. But she really *is* quite grown up ; and she is too pretty for anything. It almost frightens me when I think of the dreadful men. I must tell thee that she seems to be very high-principled, and we must all be careful not to shock her with our adult, easy-going principles. She is at the age when compromises are inadmissible.

Petty little savings in the kitchen are not going to effect much, and life is not worth living if you have got to weigh your meat and measure your milk ; and I strongly advise thee not to undertake it. Servants *always* cheat—not necessarily from dishonesty, but generally, I believe, from the sort of carelessness that is inevitable to human nature when dealing with the property of their employers. It is really only their own things that average human nature can be trusted to take honest care of. And no amount of watching can protect you from this inevitable carelessness.

To her daughter, Mary Berenson

Aet. 72.

LONDON, *April* 15, 1904

I cannot help thinking how dreadful it is for old people to go on living as we all are, doing no good to ourselves or anybody else, and being nothing but a bother and a care to everybody around us. For myself there is an excuse in the need of having a home for the children, but there is no excuse whatever for the others. Alas ! there is nobody else to take the care of old Mrs. H. but her daughter, and she has simply got to stand it, and die of it if she must. May I be preserved from ever being such a drag on anyone ! Why are such old people allowed to live on anyhow ? It has given me a horror of all old people, myself included.

I am *thankful* that thee can enjoy being with me. Thy too flattering letter came last evening, and I felt quite bashful about reading it out to the children. Well, while you *think* me nice, perhaps you will mind-cure me into being nice. I feel as if everybody ought to avoid old people as if they were the plague ! Sometime thee must tell me just what old people ought to do to make themselves agreeable. To me thy visit was heavenly.

Karin amused me greatly at lunch to-day by telling me all about how she and Mary Worthington are beginning all of a sudden to feel grown up. I tried to find out what the symptoms are and finally she said, " Well, for one thing we are beginning to think the river looks beautiful in moonlight and to like to look at it, and a little while ago we should have thought it was all rot."

What a speech about her hat for Mrs. B. to make at her child's funeral ! Not but what other people sometimes think of their clothes at funerals, but everybody else has the sense to keep their thoughts to themselves.

To her daughter, Mary Berenson

Aet. 72.

We have got along wonderfully in moving to this flat without thee, though of course thee would have been a great help. Alys is a perfect *magician* in moving. I cannot imagine that a troop of angels could have done it better. To think of it—she has emptied Friday's Hill and 44, Grosvenor Road, and got me all settled in here, and all in 10 days ! It seems like a miracle ! I have the most delicious corner, far nicer than the one in Grosvenor Road, and to be all on one floor is perfectly delightful. I can never thank thee enough for bringing it to a point. Tell B. B. it was one of the best jobs of thy life. Thee did thy share in making things easy for me ; and I do not believe any Mother ever had two better daughters. Not having any ructions of any kind has made it easier, and not having any *man* to please has conduced to this ! !

In contrast to poor Mrs. B., I sit and chuckle over the deliverance from care and from the necessity of doing anything which my lameness gives me, and rejoice at the happy prospect ahead of me. She has all the misery of old age and none of the fun, while I am determined to get all the fun out of it I can, and I find plenty.

We had such a funny talk yesterday on Art. N. expressed her admiration of a certain picture, and Ray and Karin sniffed. I told N. not to mind their sniffs, as they had been taught by their mother not to enjoy the things natural to their age, but only things old students enjoyed, and I thought it was a pity. " Yes,"

said Karin, " I often think mother makes a mistake in
not letting us enjoy things suited to our youngness, and
in making us stretch up to things we are really too
young to enjoy ! "   And then she added, " But when
she once says anything, we can't help thinking the same.
For instance, she once said that pictures were like holes
in the wall, and now whenever I look at pictures I only
see great holes in the walls, and it seems a pity."   I
advise thee to consider this youthful bit of wisdom.

To her daughter, Mary Berenson

Aet. 72.

LONDON, *Oct.* 27, 1904

I see thee expresses sentimental feelings of melancholy
over our leaving our house in Grosvenor Road !   I am
glad to say I have not a feel, except the feeling of thankfulness at having got away from that incubus of a house,
which my lameness made only a burden.   Somehow
in looking back, I seem to see myself a poor lame turtle
so weighed down by an enormous shell, that I could not
twist my poor head around to see properly, let alone to
keep in order as it should be kept.

But what exactly are thy feelings ?   I am really
curious to know.   Be sure to tell me, and maybe I can
get them up.   But define them and let me see whether
they are really genuine, or only some of A. L.'s senti-
mentalities.   I feel thankful every minute that I am in
this flat, and that I have got rid of 44 for ever.   My new
shell can never be such a burden.   In fact it feels very
light and most easy to manage.   But it really seems as
if one could hardly turn around without paying somebody for it.

N

Nov. 10, 1904

Ray says to tell thee that Oscar Wilde's article could not have any influence on her as it is so evidently intended for ridiculous nonsense, but it is very funny. I do not think she is old enough to be really hurt by it. I have read it, and cannot get much out of it except that some sort of an idea seems to glimmer through it that if one *could* keep young always and could people the world with Dragons and Fairies, and all sorts of impossible things, it would make a splendid world of it. And I believe that is what religion does for people. It fills life with delicious things, unseen by the multitude and impossible to their comprehension. I wonder if Oscar Wilde did not have a glimpse of this sometimes ? One of my greatest " openings " into the mystery of religion came from something I heard him say in Philadelphia, dressed in shorts with a big sunflower in his buttonhole. He said, " You can conquer a city by force, but you can only conquer the Art of that city by submission to its rules."

To her daughter, Mary Berenson

Aet. 72.

LONDON, *Nov.* 12, 1904

The children and I were very much interested at breakfast this morning by thy description of the " feelings " about the house in Grosvenor Road, and Karin said, " But, grandma, even if you don't *feel* those feelings, you ought to sympathise with them." I could only say that I considered them a useless bother, and consequently never encouraged them. The truth is I am like the Apostle—always reaching out towards the things that are before, and forgetting the things that are behind. (See Phil. III. 13, 14.) And I always find new things so much better than old ones that it seems pure waste of time to mourn over the old.

This room is so light and airy compared to my old room at 44, that that one seems like a sort of prison cell from which I have made a happy escape, and to waste my energies regretting it, would seem to me the height of folly. And nothing suits me better than to say of things that they are done with forever. Life seems to me like a pilgrimage to a longed-for country, and I welcome the passage of every stage as so much gained towards the blissful end, and *cannot* be sorry that they have passed. I wonder if thee can understand *my* feelings any better than I can understand *thine* ?

This morning I asked Ray and Karin if they had any " feelings " about No. 44, and Ray said most emphatically, " No, not the least scrap." " But," she added, " if you were to ask me about Friday's Hill, I had and still have oceans and I could weep tears of sorrow any minute over having to leave it." Then Karin joined in and said she sometimes felt a little sentimental about No. 44, but when she thought of Friday's Hill, all her sentiments left No. 44, and went over in a body to Friday's Hill. Has thee any feelings about Friday's Hill ? I have none.

At breakfast this morning Karin said, " Grandma, I have discovered at my age that the expectation of a thing is generally nicer than the thing itself. Somehow the thing itself never seems to come up to one's expectations." I said, " Thee is growing older, Karin." " Yes," she said, " I am afraid I am, and I keep making that kind of discovery ; and it can't *all* be my getting into the Sixth Form ; it must be age as well."

To Miss Olive Seward [1]

LONDON, *Nov.* 28, 1904

I am indeed proud of being an American, although I must confess to a little weakness towards being an American living in London ! Did I tell thee that we are living right alongside of the Westminster Cathedral ? It is delightful for Ray and Karin, and I can hear the singing up through my windows, and can see the Holy Fathers taking their exercise on the flat roofs of the various buildings connected with the Cathedral. It gives quite an air of sanctity to the whole atmosphere, for they do look so good.

To her daughter, Mary Berenson

Aet. 72.

LONDON, *Jan.* 1, 1905

I *shall* be glad to see thee back, daughter, for I miss thee dreadfully. I wish I did not ! I was taking a nap in my chair to-day, and I thought I heard thee rustling thy papers, and I looked over at thy table expecting to see thee, and alas ! thee was not there, and it was dreadful.

I consider the burden of debt is an almost unbearable one, and if I could once get free from it, I feel as if I should hide myself in some little cottage in the depths of a forest where it would be impossible for me ever to make another debt all my life long. A horrid demand for taxes has just come in. It is harrowing.

Tell B. B. that my most successful book [*The Christian's Secret*] was written so to speak at the point of the

[1] The adopted daughter of William Henry Seward, Abraham Lincoln's Secretary of State.

bayonet, without one ray of enthusiasm, and *hating* to do it all the time. So he may be encouraged.

To her daughter, Mary Berenson

Aet. 73.

LONDON, *Feb.* 22, 1905

Yes, we did rejoice in the assassination of the Grand Duke,[1] and we only hope there will be some more ! I have always said that Quaker or no Quaker, if I had lived in Russia, I should have been a Nihilist ! It is the only voice the people have. I will get that National Review and read that article, but I am afraid it will make me more furious than is comfortable.

Feb. 25, 1905

I must repeat that I *did* write " The Christian's Secret " at the point of the bayonet, as it were. I did not want to write it at all, and only did it at father's earnest entreaties. He had started a Paper, which I thought was a great mistake, and I declared I would not write a line for it. But he begged so hard that at last I said I would write one article and no more, if he would give up drinking wine at dinner. Then when that article was published everybody clamoured for another, and father begged, and I was good-natured and went on, but under a continual protest. And the best chapter of all was written on a voyage over from America to England, when I was sea-sick all the time, and as near cursing as a person who had experienced the " blessings of holiness " could dare to be ! So tell B. B. books can be successful even if they

[1] The reactionary Grand-duke Sergius who, during the Russian troubles, had been assassinated on Feb. 4.

are ground out with groans and curses, and I feel very hopeful of his book.   The great point is to have something to say, and this he has.

I enclose thee a sample of Ray's Mathematics that thee may get a little idea of what the child is doing. It seems incredible that this is the child of whom thee and I felt very doubtful whether she could ever learn to eat a bun !

I wish I could give thee my philosophy of life which has carried me through my 70 years without any serious quarrels with anyone, and has given me the universal reputation of being a peacemaker.   Even through all the mazes of theological controversy, which is quite as quarrelsome a matter as " Kunst-fussing ", I always managed to be at peace with my opponents, and I cannot remember ever having had what I considered an enemy, although others might have thought I ought to have considered them as such.   And as a fact some of my apparently worst enemies have become in the end my warmest friends.

I came across a book that taught that the true secret of the philosophy of Jesus was to become a King by being the Servant of all, and it carried such profound conviction to my soul that I have always tried to act on it.   It struck me as being not so much religion as the most profound common-sense.   And such it has proved to be throughout my whole life.   Even through all the fights in the Women's Christian Temperance Union and the British Women's, it has worked with almost magical power.

The girls went to Confession last evening, so had to get up early to go to Church before breakfast this morning.   It seems a bother, but I feel it is more of a comfort than a bother, for to have your conscience cleared and all your sins cast into the depths of oblivion once a month would certainly be very conducive to one's peace of mind, if one could only believe in it, as no doubt they do. And fortunately there is nothing *contrary* to my religion in it, although it does not quite go to the length of mine. For I believe you can do the same thing every day, or every hour, or whenever you feel a need, and that too without the intervention of any Confessional Box or any Holy Father. To me the Box and the Father would be nothing but a hindrance, but to many people no doubt a tangible Box and a materialised Father are genuine helps, and I have no fault to find with them.

Babies *are* fun, but I am done with them, thank goodness.

To her daughter, Mary Berenson

Aet. 73.

LONDON, *April* 26, 1905

Being lifted in and out of the motor will be a work, but as I am not sure I can see Alys's new home by looking over the ramparts of Heaven, I think I must try and do it while I am down here.

Thy letter made me shake in my shoes a little. Human nature *is* human nature, even in such exceedingly young specimens as Ray and Willy. And when I cast my mind back to the year 1850, and remember what a silly ignorant creature *I* was, and how Cupid entrapped *me*, I cannot consider any amount of youthfulness or ignorance a safeguard. And when I think of THEE ! ! Words are wanting to express my fears !

How lovely of Ray to be so appreciative of me and of the love by which they have been surrounded. I certainly am on their side more than I am on my own, and this I believe is the real nature of true love. If people only could realise that this is the nature of God's love !

It is very funny, but now that Ray is away, I keep looking out for all the girls of about her age, and with frocks about as long as hers, as I drive along in old Rollings, and my heart goes out to every one.

Thee has my hearty sympathy in thy discovery of the fact that young people *do not care*, as a general thing, for the things that interest their elders. Ray is where she always has been and where we have known her to be, frankly indifferent to sight-seeing, and making no pretence to be anything different. But for any awkward reserve to come between thee and Ray would be grievous. And there is not the slightest need, if only you will both be frank. If thee wants Ray to look at anything, tell her so, and, if she doesn't want to look at it, let her say so frankly, and then thee let it drop. When you go to Venice ask her plump out whether she would rather see Churches, or swim at the Lido, and, as no doubt she will choose the Lido, the Lido let it be.

To her daughter, Mary Berenson

Aet. 73.

LONDON, *May 22*, 1905

Hurrah for Ray ! She is a girl after my own heart ! As to *thee* with thy match-making propensities, I can only say it is a mercy thee has a daughter who can outwit thee !

May 24, 1905

I actually begin to suspect that thee *did* look upon Willy in the light of a " parti " for Ray ! ! It seems impossible that thee could have wanted her to be " caught " at this early age, after thy own experiences in the matter, and above all that thee could want her to go out to Pittsburgh to live ! Do tell me whether I am Libelling thee by such suspicions. But I do believe that thy flirting tendencies are now turned into flirtations for thy daughter, and that if Ray was not endowed with some of my good sense, acquired by sore experience, she would surely be entrapped.

I quite enjoyed a visit from the three Pearsall aunts but *you* with your subtleties of conversation, would have been bored to extinction. I warned Alys not to come near us to-day, as there is no reason she should be drawn into such a boring net.

June 7, 1905

How I should have enjoyed your trip to Lucca myself ! But I mean to make up for what I have missed in this line by going off on a Star or astride the tail of a Comet when I get to Heaven, and exploring the circumambient Universe ! Ha, Ha !

To her daughter, Mary Berenson

Aet. 73.

LONDON, *Sept.* 19, 1905

The journey up to Town from High Buildings was satisfactorily accomplished. Edmund's van took me beautifully in my chair, and we had an old door of the

barn to roll me up on, with Edmund and Logan pushing on each side.

When I think of my old activities it really seems
incredible that it should be for me that such arrangements were necessary. I felt as if I were some other
decrepit old individual who had no business to take
journeys anyhow. Then at the station I was lifted
into the luggage van, and Alys and Ray took turns
keeping me company. At Vauxhall they carried me
to a cab in a carrying chair and I managed with Alys's
help to get in, and felt at home in Rolling's old 4-
wheeler. The porter gave me a welcome, and we
were soon up in our flat, and my table was all ready
for me to be wheeled straight to it. At last I begin to
feel settled, and my sacred disorder begins to look like
itself.

We miss thee more than words can say, but it is not
profitable to enlarge on this topic.

I am dipped into sympathy with thee over the dress
question. I confess it does seem to be a dreadful waste
of time and money, and, worse still, of brains and of
temper too, to turn your mortal frame into a dressmaker's block, and I cannot help thinking it must be
deteriorating to the character. Do assert thy independence and cut loose from it all. Suppose I had
devoted my life to such things, what sort of a creature
would I be now?

Personally I could not endure such boring visits as
you suffer a single day; but then I am not good at
standing bores, my legs get into such dreadful fidgets,
and nearly everybody bores me nowadays, all except
my own family and Grace.

To her daughter, Mary Berenson

Aet. 73.

LONDON, *Oct.* 16, 1905

Of all hateful occupations, housekeeping is to my mind the most hateful. Nurse was just like poor Mrs. Truilzi in this, that she *would* parade all the faults and all the peculiarities of the other servants before me day after day ; and therefore I know well how thoroughly disagreeable it is. Logan's attitude is the right one, " If the house is on fire, don't tell me." But alas ! the housekeeper must not say this, but must watch every spark, and must trample it out, and it is *not* agreeable. But I hope things will brighten with thee in a few days, or at any rate thee will get on a rhinoceros skin that won't care. Thank goodness I have no man to cater for !

I am dressed up in my best now, awaiting the coming of poor weeping Lady Low, and two of her friends who have read my books and are coming to see my wings.

If thee could only settle down to noises as being part of the ordained order of things, they would not disturb thee. I hear no noises here at night at all when thee is not here, but, as soon as thee comes, I am so afraid of thy being disturbed, that I hear them all the time. Or rather I should say that I hear them but do not notice them in the least except when thee is here. Do put thy will power into this, and when noises come, just say to thyself not " How can I stop it ", or " how annoying it is ", or anything, except just " It is none of my business ", and turn over and ignore it. I know that *can* be done.

Nov. 15, 1905

Our dressmaker, poor Miss Larby's, love affair, which has experienced various ups and downs, has come to an end this evening, by a letter from the man saying it was only a flirtation, and she must not think of it any more. It is a disappointment, but I tell her he probably has a wife somewhere else, and it is a happy escape for her.

To her daughter, Mary Berenson

Aet. 73.

LONDON, *Nov.* 17, 1905

Almost any school with a lot of girls would be more fun for Karin than your grown-up (not to say middle-aged) atmosphere. Look at Ray, what bliss all the nonsensical fun they have at Newnham is to her. It is evidently the divine order, and there is no getting out of it. They must have their fun just as kittens must, and not with their mothers, but with other kittens.

I tremble in my bed at the thought of thy sleeping arrangements here. The Flat over us is taken by an American Actress and her mother. They seem to *me* very quiet, but I suppose to thee they will seem like raging bulls.

I do wonder if a procession of all the people I have helped will come to meet me when I enter Heaven! Or will they have discovered that I had got everything wrong and had only hindered them instead of helping, and so come to try and persuade Peter to shut the gate against me! It will be rather interesting to see. I have just had sent me a translation of one of my tracts, and the title is " All bugsvalelses

Gad ", meaning " The God of all Comfort ".   What a language ! It is Swedish.   What do those barbarians mean by a " fat nose " ?   It *cannot* be the same meaning we would have.

Thee need not feel the slightest delicacy about always telling me how B. B. feels.   My experience of life has taught me to look upon the vagaries of the male portion of our race as one looks upon avalanches or earthquakes—things that cannot be stopped nor altered, but must simply have way made for them, with as little personal inconvenience to one's self as possible.   And just as one would always be glad to know when avalanches or earthquakes are coming, so I always like to know what the men of my acquaintance feel about things, or what they want, in order that I may get out of the way.

I am afraid Willie's continual smoking has so undermined his moral nature that he really does not know right from wrong, poor fellow.

To her daughter, Mary Berenson

Aet. 74.

LONDON, *Feb.* 15, 1906

I send thee a belated birthday present—a telescope Cigarette holder.   Thee need not advertise that it is a present from the author of the " Christian's Secret of a Happy Life " !   But I think it may save thee from a little of the poison of thy cigarettes, of which I have a few fears.

I sympathise with thee from the bottom of my heart over your guests, for I know it well from many experiences of incompetent Missionaries with their still more incompetent wives, who were foisted on me by poor father's unthinking hospitality, and all their burdens rolled over off his shoulders on to mine. But Mother Smith showed me the way out at last, and that was never to take them *into our own house*, to upset everything and make everybody uncomfortable, but to arrange for them to go into lodgings near by, where I could see them as often as necessary, but from where I could escape to the peace and quiet of my own home.

It is really kinder to the people themselves too ; whereas, while they are in your house, they will simply lie back and depend altogether on you. At present thee is pauperising those poor dear people, and it is thy duty to force them to work for their own living. I think thee ought to find them lodgings and tell them thee cannot get a villa for them, nor a servant, nor oversee their affairs, as thee makes it a rule not to do things like that for other people. (Make the rule quick, now, as thee reads this letter.)

To her daughter, Mary Berenson

Aet. 74.

LONDON, *Feb.* 22, 1906

I do not wonder thee was " jiggered " over that cigarette case. I felt rather jiggered myself. But as thee is too old for me to forbid thee to smoke, and so I am entirely delivered from responsibility, I want, since thee *will* smoke, to help thee to do it as comfortably as possible. I do not understand it, unless it is that the mother in me gets the better of the reformer sometimes ! And I happened to see that little holder at one of those moments. Such are the frailties of poor human nature !

I feel quite awed at the thought of Ray being nineteen so soon.   When I was 19 I got married, like the ignorant idiot I was.   And what worries me is that I had no more thought of doing such a thing than she has, and had not the slightest fondness for men.   It all came on me like the earthquake on San Francisco last week, and in one day my life was overturned.   And why may it not be the same with Ray ?   It would be *too* awful !

We have all been Suffra-ging this morning.   I went in Rollings with placards on each door, " Votes for Women ", and a badge fastened on to my bonnet in front, and Alys and Grace and Mary and Mrs. Rollings and Miss Larby all walked in the procession alongside.

Grace and I felt the greatest sympathy with thy wail this morning.   I have long wondered how thee can stand the boring visitors thee has.   I could not possibly do it, I have kept clear of bores all my life long by judiciously pulling out my watch, when the boring stage was reached, and saying, " I am afraid I shall have to go to my work," or " I am afraid I must go out," or something.   This gets you up a character for being hard at work, and people are impressed rather than annoyed.

Your trip sounds heavenly.   Would that such things had happened in my day !   Still, I have had a good share of fun in my life, and one region I have at least partly explored that beats all of yours, and that when once you have got into it, becomes your permanent residence, and no man can take it from you !

But I myself am having so many visitors just now that I can hardly get time to write.   It is my last book that has stirred them to come for help.   It is to be hoped I give them sound teaching !   At any rate it is *comfortable* teaching.

July 23, 1906

My stream of company goes on streaming. Somebody especial for private interviews is coming every afternoon until I go to the country. Yesterday Lady Rosslyn was here, and Gertrude Mallet came. Whenever I get anyone who *professes* to believe the Bible, I give them no quarter until they really do accept it as true, or else deny it altogether. It is absurd to keep saying they believe God loves them, and all the while thinking He doesn't. Any idiot can be made to see this.

But here comes another—and I must close. This one is a Missionary from America.

Karin can go to Confession on Saturday night and to early Mass on Sunday, and so be free for a month. (To think that Hannah Whitall Smith should have to write such words !)

To her granddaughter, Ray Costelloe

Aet. 74.

COURT PLACE, IFFLEY, *Nov.* 14, 1906

I long to know, Ray, whether thy yellow dress filled up a " long felt want ", or whether it turned to ashes on thy back.

In thy Debate in favour of Motoring, thee can extinguish thy opponents by gently reminding them of the opposition railroads met with at first. They were considered a wicked tempting of Providence. And thee can tell them when sewing machines first came in they were looked upon as the offspring of Hell. Even thy grandmother (myself) had to hide one she bought in her attic and keep it a profound secret, because her friends thought it was such a sinful machine.

And in thy great-grandmother's day suspenders to hold up men's trousers were believed to be invented by Satan !

I left London forever without a pang, and, to tell the whole truth, without a single " feel " of any sort or description.

To Miss Olive Seward

Aet. 74.

IFFLEY, *Jan.* 27, 1907

Thy letter of December was a great joy to me, and it was answered in my heart at once. But my writer's cramp makes writing very difficult, and my hand so soon tires that I find myself unable to do more than attend to my necessary correspondence, and all else has to wait. To-day I feel a little more limber than usual, and must try and send thee at least a few lines. It was delightful to get into touch with thee again, and to know something of thy whereabouts and of thy life. And it is a joy to know that, no matter how far separated nor how long our silences, we always meet on the same old terms and find ourselves unaltered towards one another. I include dear mystical Sara [1] in this, and I love to think of her mystical musings and of the beatific visions I am sure she has ; although I alas ! cannot share them. I say alas, because they have always been unattainable experiences to me for, like thee, the practical, and what William James calls the " pragmatical " side of religion has always seemed to suit me best. Thee and I, beloved Olive, were rather choked off, I think, by the strong doses we shared together in the long ago years, and now I can heartily unite with thee in feeling that plain simple

[1] Sara Lipton, who lived with Olive Seward.

O

common-sense faith is the strongest staff upon which one can safest lean.

But I must tell thee about my move here. The occasion of it was that my two granddaughters who had always lived with me, had grown up and were away, one at College and one at school, and I was left alone ; and as neither Mariechen nor Alys could be with me, and Logan greatly preferred Oxford to London, we decided that I had far better take up my abode with him there, especially as he seems destined to be an old bachelor. He found this place on the banks of the river, next door to the beautiful Iffley Church, which I am sure thee must have seen. We have about eight acres and some splendid old trees, among the rest a magnificent Cedar of Lebanon. Out of the window where I am sitting to write, I look across green lawns to the river, and can see a little white footbridge over which Alys bicycles almost every day to see me.

I am very happy here, and although I am confined to my wheeled chair and cannot get out much, yet the views out of our windows are so lovely, and the river is so shining, and the grass is so green, that I feel the lines have indeed fallen to me in pleasant places. I often have a feeling as if I were living in a novel, and this is a distinct charm of entering into the life of another country from your own. I have it here, whenever I stop to realise that I am living on the banks of the river Thames.

To her daughter, Mary Berenson
Aet. 74. IFFLEY, *Feb.* 2, 1907

I wonder if you *ought* to urge B. B. to write when he feels so unable to do it. If you spur him on too far, all his machinery may give out, and thee may have him a helpless invalid on thy hands. Let him lie absolutely fallow for awhile ; and then, if he has any-thing to say, and any power to say it, he will feel an inspiration, and it will be easy. I read a very striking story once of a man with a great deal of brain power, whose wife urged him on and on to do a certain piece of work when he felt unequal to it, and as a result his brain gave way, and he was a semi-idiot the rest of his life—I advise thee to be careful, but do not tell B. B. all this.

Mar. 5, 1907

I am dreadfully distressed by thy attack of shingles. Do ask Mr. Cannon whether he suffered with neuralgia after his attack. If he did probably his present suffer-ings have been caused by it. Doctor Osler says in his Medical book that that sort of neuralgia sometimes lasts for years. How old was Mr. Cannon when he had his attack ? As for thee, thee is far too young for such an infliction. And just here let me advise thee not to talk of thyself as being *old*. There *is* something in Mind Cure, after all, and, if thee continually talks of thyself as being old, thee may perhaps bring on some of the infirmities of age. At least I would not risk it if I were thee.

The drawing-room blinds have come, and are a lovely light green, and harmonise beautifully with the greenish tinge of the walls. I receive my callers in there now, and I feel myself exactly like a fasting man in a glass case, on show.

Thee suggests that Logan and I are becoming " County " people, but thee is very much mistaken. The " County " never call on the Iffley " gentry " (so-called). No, we are only middle class, perhaps upper, but I don't know yet. But, County, Upper, or Lower, I feel perfectly indifferent, for my world is apart from them all. And my only desire is not to be bothered with any of them, except when they have had Shingles.

I believe when you are tempted to be cross it is a great help just to say to your friends, " I know I am going to be cross, but you must not mind it, for it is only disease." Somehow this seems to relieve the strain.

To her daughter, Mary Berenson

Aet. 75.

IFFLEY, *May* 30, 1907

Another caller ! It really is dreadful to be so the prey of callers. I do not see how I am going to stand it. It was very different in London, for all my visitors there came for religious talks in which I was really interested, and here it is all surface talk which I hate.

The invitations for our garden party have gone out ; and now comes the problem of what is to become of *me* ; for, according to present appearances, I shall have to spend all my time wheeling back and forth to and from my Commode, and I do not exactly see how that is going to fit into a Garden Party ! ! Perhaps I had better receive my guests enthroned on it in state ! ! I shall not expect you, as there really is no need, and there is certainly no enjoyment. I have all my life long found social functions an unmitigated bore.

June 5, 1907

My Shingles are developing more and more sores, and I think the prospects are that when the Garden Party arrives, Mrs. Pearsall Smith will have to be

hidden upstairs. I could not stand the " gay world " [1]
here, if I had to visit ; and I am thankful for my
wheeled chair every day of my life.

June 20

My sores are much better, and I think I can appear
at the Garden Party without causing a shudder of
disgust to sweep through the company. But it does
seem a pity I cannot look my prettiest.

To her daughter, Mary Berenson

Aet. 75.

IFFLEY, *Sept.* 21, 1907

I have just heard that Edward Clifford is dead !
It is a great shock, as, although I knew he was gradually
failing, I had no idea he was so near death. He was
my faithful and quite devoted friend for 40 years, and
I shall miss him a good deal, but I am awfully glad for
him.

I do hope that B. B. will not succeed in turning thee
into a milliner's block. You cannot dress in the
height of fashion without one of two things :—either
you must pour out money like water, or else you must
give all your time and energies to it ; and I should
hate to see thee doing either of these things. It seems
to me such an ignoble pursuit for anyone with good
sense.

I am not *the least* lonely, honest Injun.

[1] To her daughter the word " gay " would have an overtone of
particular and moral significance : " By ' gay ' we meant anything
that was not Quakerly. Quakers were ' plain ' and all the rest of the
world, and even of the Church, was ' gay '." (*The Unselfishness of God*,
p. 51.) This special sense of the word might cover anything almost,
from the Lord's Prayer to the use of sewing machines.

To her daughter, Mary Berenson

Aet. 75.

IFFLEY, *Oct.* 15, 1907

Well, I accomplished my eulogy of Edward Clifford yesterday afternoon, and feel enormously relieved. But I had no idea I was as " pious " as I found myself to be, for I could not remember any of my intercourse with him except that on the spiritual plane. All our intercourse on the earthly plane seems to have faded away into a misty distance, while the other is as fresh and vivid as possible.

It is cold and rainy this morning, and I have put on under-vest no. 3—one of those knitted woollen ones, and feel in consequence lovely and warm. When it gets colder, I will put on no. 4, and with four under-vests, a pair of corded corsets, a corset cover, a dress waist, and a velveteen bolero jacket, altogether eight coverings, to say nothing of my rolls of fat, I shall, I trust, be able to defy the winter. See how sensible I am, and take example thereby. If I should still feel the cold, I shall not hesitate to put on no. 9 and no. 10 for warm and comfortable I *intend* to be ! I feel like an animated cushion, as if pins might be stuck into me anywhere, and never succeed in pricking me.

Again callers have hindered my writing. I believe Iffley people spend their lives paying calls ! However, I nearly converted one of my callers to Suffrage for women, and Logan and the other lady had a free fight about Free Trade. I do not feel as well up in Free Trade as in Suffrage. There *may* be two sides to the first, but to the last there is and can be only one. Of that I am sure.

This evening Logan is going into Oxford to hear

Bertie Russell lecture on Pragmatism. I wish I could hear him. I expect he will tear it to pieces.

To her daughter, Mary Berenson
Aet. 75.

IFFLEY, *Nov.* 15, 1907

Poor dear Emily—her illness is *too* dreadful, and I am afraid she has no religion to comfort her. You people without religion have no idea what a dreadful loss it is. Instead of its being meritorious on the part of anyone to believe in the God of the New Testament, it is the greatest piece of self-indulgence possible, for there is no comfort in the universe to equal it.

We are eager to hear the details of the Cyclopean quarrel between the Thorolds and the Hapgoods. What a place Florence is for quarrels! I begin to think it is some sort of microbe. Do watch that you don't become infected.

I am going to read Logan's Life of Sir Henry Wotton [1] sometime when I can find *time* to do it leisurely, and see if I can discover its beauties. If only it would ever be possible for thee and me to read it together, we might stir each other up to a greater admiration than we have at present. But do not say anything to Logan about this. My nausea is all right again to-day. It was evidently the green corn I had been eating. (But it *was* good!)

I do seem to have a great press of business just now. Bessie Taylor has applied to me to help her prepare a life of grandpa Whitall for young Friends. Lady Henry has applied to help her with her life of Miss Willard. My publisher has applied to know whether

[1] *The Life and Letters of Sir Henry Wotton,* in two volumes, by Logan Pearsall Smith. Oxford: Clarendon Press, 1907.

a gentleman may print one of the chapters of the " Christian's Secret " as a tract. A lady from South Africa writes to know whether she has committed the unpardonable sin etc. etc. Lady Rosslyn writes to ask me to read an article on Socialism by her daughter, Lady Warwick, and tell her what I think of it. And so on and so on, until I hardly get time to read my papers.

To her daughter, Mary Berenson

Aet. 75.

IFFLEY, *Dec.* 1, 1907

I confess I have had a great many secret misgivings as to your settling down in an English country house, on account of the loneliness and dreariness of winter. It struck me like a pall when we went to see Wood Eaton. I did not say anything, because I did not want to discourage any chance of getting you over here, but I inwardly decided that it would take a house *full* of interesting people to make it a pleasant winter home. I am very much afraid you would not like it over here for long ; and your having a home in Italy would not prevent your taking a house in England, either in the country or in London, for as long or short a time as you might like.

Of course it would be *lovely* to have you near me, but it would be unwise to count on that, for I do not intend to live any longer than I can help, and at any moment I might get dotty, and be anything but a pleasure to be with. And as I say, you can always take a house near me while I am at all desirable as a companion.

But in spite of my Bladder trouble, I have not felt at all weak or sick to-day. It does not seem to affect my general health at all, which is discouraging from the point of view of Heaven, and just at present, although it would be *delicious* to have thee, I do not really need thee ; and I should be so afraid of upsetting thee by my discomforts and my miseries that I should have to pretend there was nothing the matter. I am really freer to groan and grumble when I am all alone ; and, a good deal of the time, I can go on with my usual pursuits. I have plenty of odd jobs to keep me busy and plenty of odd naps to take between times.

I *am* thankful thee did not tell Karin about Mme von H. It is a disastrous thing to weaken the moral sense in young people by familiarity with delightful immoral people ; and I confess that I dread Italy for Ray and Karin more on this account than on any other. Older people, whose moral nature is already more or less settled, may not be hurt by it perhaps, though even this is doubtful ; but young people, whose moral character is being formed are almost certainly bound to be deteriorated by it, and can hardly help coming to grief.

To her daughter, Mary Berenson

Aet. 75.

IFFLEY, *Jan.* 31, 1908

I have been wondering, in view just now of the fact that you are so enthusiastic over the " young ", why it is that you exalt youth on such a high pedestal. I do not remember ever feeling it was such a great achievement to be young, and such a matter of deep regret to be growing old ; and I have never been able to understand your feelings in the matter. But I think I have solved it at last. It is because to you this life is all, you do not believe in a future life that is to be the crown and fulfilment of this ; and naturally to grow old is to you a disaster that has no alleviations ; while to me growing old in this life only means a day by day nearer approach to the entrance upon another life far higher and grander than this life is or ever could be ; and naturally I am in a hurry to get there.

Feeling as good for nothing as I do, and the certainty that all earthly things must necessarily one by one fall away from me, I should indeed be miserable if this life were all. I seem to have got a glimpse into the misery and desolation of a life without God and without a future, that fills me with the most profound sympathy for you. Whatever thee does, darling daughter, do not, I entreat of thee, deprive thy daughters of whatever faith they may have, even though it should be the narrowest Catholicism, by any influence of thine.

The Zangwills have just come. They seem very nice, but I am going to take advantage of my invalidism, and see very little of them.

Feb. 1, 1908

I am delighted to know that thee realises the absolute necessity of keeping Ray and Karin as ignorant of the evils in the world as thee can ; and I must say that I rejoice that Ray *is* a little priggish. It will need some priggishness to keep her straight in the atmosphere of Italy.

To her daughter, Mary Berenson
Aet. 75.

IFFLEY, *Feb.* 5, 1908

Alas for maternity—how it hurts, and what agonies for mothers lie hidden in the fate of our children !

Here are both Ray and Karin not well at Newnham, and I feel as if I would like to upset the whole order of the universe to make them well again.

I had a worshipper here to-day, a lady who came out to see about taking Grace's cottage. She found out that I was *the* Mrs. Pearsall Smith, and she begged so hard to be allowed just to look on my face, that Logan had to bring her into my sitting-room, and then what did she do but actually kneel down and seize my hand and kiss it, and weep, so speechless with emotion that she could only ejaculate, " To think I should have this inestimable privilege ! " etc. etc. till I was ready to shake her. It was most embarrassing.

I really began to feel a sympathy with God for the worship He has to put up with so often ! Logan fled from the room ; and I managed to get the poor dear soul up on to a chair, and quieted her down a little. But I felt a wretch for being so unsympathetic, and I expect she felt sadly disappointed not to see more signs of a halo and wings ! I shall have to protect myself from her adorations somehow, but I am afraid she will set me wild. You will all have to protect me.

To her daughter, Mary Berenson

Aet. 76.

IFFLEY, *Feb.* 14, 1908

This is a happy anniversary for me, thy birthday. Love, as thee feels it for Ray and Karin, is purely heavenly and does smooth out everything. But passion is purely material or earthly, what the Bible calls carnal, and it truly does confuse everything. It is a horrid (although sometimes entrancing) element.

We are all absorbed this afternoon in the fall of the

big tree we are having cut down. I told thee yesterday that they were at work on it, and the critical moment of its final fall has now arrived. When it is down, it will give us a splendid view of the Cedar of Lebanon.

It is down—hurrah !

The wild life at Sandgate suits Karin exactly, and she thinks it would be bliss to get once more into that " Pirate Band ", and roam the country at night unhindered. This Pirate Band is composed of four young men, and Margaret, and Hester, and Karin, each one wilder than the other, except that I have no doubt our beloved Karin is the wildest of all, with her wild Irish blood, the darling.

I should like to see Karin dressed as Byron. Does she know his poetry ? Does thee ? I do not think I ever read a line, for when I was young and cared for poetry, Byron was considered too " gay " for young Quakers to read. Is it not rather immoral in its tendencies ?

I should love to be present at one of your Santa Conversaziones. I wonder if I could understand you, or is my outlook so widely different from yours that all your talk would be worse than Greek to me that did understand what thee said about the secret of successful novel writing to Ray—namely that the making of real characters is the one essential. I know from experience that the novels I have really enjoyed, and that have left the strongest impression on me are those that have made me acquainted with a real person, and have given me an actual new friend. I would carry it further and say that to make a place real, or the circumstances of the story real are also most important. I know some of Mrs. Oliphant's books have done this for me, and have left me with a sort of inner consciousness that I have made a new friend and have visited a new country, and shall always have them both in remembrance.

I have never yet seen, either indoors or out, a pretty woman in Oxford.

To her daughter, Mary Berenson

Aet. 76.

IFFLEY, *April* 15, 1908

I should be only too delighted if I could believe thee really did adore B. B.[1] It is such a rare trait in a wife that I could hardly believe it ; but, if it is true, thee could not have a more secure foundation for happiness. But I must confess that the sort of life you lead, with such a continual procession of visitors, would be weariness beyond words to me, and it is a continual amazement to me that you stand it. The talk must necessarily be mostly on the surface of things, and to me nothing is more wearisome. That is why I hate the English calling business so much. It certainly is an utter waste of life. But I suppose you could not easily get out of it, so you must try and make it profitable somehow, either to yourselves or to your friends.

My plan of life has been to avoid as far as possible all *useless* efforts, and to have real enjoyment or real profit for somebody in all that I go in for. But you have to keep out of the mere conventionalities to accomplish this. And if I was in a position where I had to return the attentions of our neighbours here, I would have to move away. I simply could not stand

---

[1] This observation, of course, has no bearing on Mr. Berenson's character, or on his mother-in-law's opinion of him (they got on well together) ; it was merely the result of a constitutional disbelief that any woman could become happy because of her marriage.

it.   I have an unfailing fortress of invalidism in which I can shut myself up.

I am sitting to-day at my table with my window open enjoying the primroses and the tulips, and thinking if all this is so lovely, how much more lovely will the life beyond be, when I am so happy as to get there.   There will be no bothersome Bladder to trouble me then !

The girls decided to play Demon in my sitting-room, and asked if I would let them say " Damn " now and then, and what could a poor foolish grandmother say but, " Yes " !   (But do not put this in my Memoirs, I beg of thee !)

P.S.   I must add a line to say that I want thee to impress on B. B. and Carlo Placci [1] that they must try to keep from waking thee up if thee should happen to fall asleep at any time.   The reason I say this is because I remember thy telling me how they sometimes blew trumpets in thy ears for a joke when thee fell asleep ;   and this is too great a risk for thee to run, both on account of thy vital need of sleep, and also on account of the danger of injuring thy ears by the loud noise.

To her daughter, Mary Berenson

Aet. 76.

IFFLEY, *May* 23, 1908

William James and his wife have been here to lunch, and Logan has just taken them to Oxford in his launch —I asked him a little about his " views ", but did not get hold of anything very satisfactory.   I could not

[1] An Italian friend of the Berensons.   A portrait of him by Mr. Berenson was published in *Horizon* for June, 1946, under the title of *A Latin Profile.*

find that he had any real foundation for his beliefs, and he certainly had no God to offer me that I could depend on. He said that I was only the *second* person who had said a word to him about his work since he came to Oxford four weeks ago. He longs to talk his philosophy over with the thinkers here, but they are all too shy to introduce the subject, and he does not like to do it himself.

To her daughter, Mary Berenson, and her grand-daughters, Ray and Karin Costelloe

Aet. 76.

IFFLEY, *Sept.* 10, 1908

It was with a heavy heart I saw you go off to America yesterday, and wheeled back after each departure, to my bright sitting-room, feeling very weepy, but quite determined to be happy in the thought of the interesting new experiences you are going into, and of the interesting life that lies before you. I confess I felt like a hen seeing its tenderly cherished chickens paddling off into unknown waters ; and I could not help asking myself whether I had been as faithful as I ought to my trust, and had prepared you to my best ability to meet the life that lies before you. But of one thing I am sure, and that is that I tried, and where I failed I can only commit you to your Heavenly Father and trust Him to make up my deficiencies. If I had given you any parting advice it would I think all have been comprised in this one sentence *to live up always to the best and highest you know.*

The grandest Christian I ever met told me that the one single rule of his life had been always to let his obedience keep pace with his light, and it had led him into a life of victory. I could enlarge for pages, but do not want to bore you, so enough said. I mean all this especially for you two young things, but my heart includes your mother also.

Great cleanings up are going on to-day. The Drawing-room is all turned out, the beds are all made up clean, the large dining table has gone out to the Coach House, and the small one has taken its place, and in a day or two Logan and I shall be reduced to our lives of dual loneliness. How we shall miss you all no words can say! But at any rate no oceans or continents can deprive me of the joys I have had in your sweet and beloved companionship in the past, nor of the hope of its renewal in the future. You all three have certainly given me more happiness in my life than ever I could tell you, and I thank you all from the bottom of my heart.

XI

THE END OF A JOURNEY

*To her daughter, Mary Berenson, and her grand-
daughters, Ray and Karin Costelloe*

Aet. 76.

This morning I had the great delight of your first
letters, which comforted my old grandmotherly heart
not a little. It is lovely to think that we have all been
a joy and comfort to one another throughout our lives
together ; and now that you young fledglings are
trying your wings, I am sure you will be no less a joy
and comfort even though henceforth I can only watch
your flights, and no longer carry you in my arms, or
guide your feet.

I tell them all photographing me is of no use, as I
know I cannot make a good picture at my age, and
I do not intend to leave behind me any picture that
is not good looking ! ! Why should I ? You all
declare I am good looking, and I want to leave behind
me proofs that you have been telling the truth !
Letters from Ray and Karin arrived this morning
declaring a state of gluttony that is hard to understand
when one sits down to tough beef, and carrots and
parsnips, and the inevitable caramel pudding. I
should enjoy a good feast of splendid big fried oysters,
I must confess, and corn, and lima beans, and egg-
plant, etc. etc.

Nov. 10, 1908

Miss Fullerton has just come home from a visit to
Henry James. He was overcome with shyness, and

I expect so was she or they never would have chosen anything so banal as *my* rheumatism to talk about ! He never seemed to be satisfied, but would go into every detail of my rheumatism and what I was doing for it, and how much it crippled me, etc. etc. Perhaps his novel, which he said he was writing, has a rheumatic heroine in it.

To her daughter, Mary Berenson

Aet. 76.

ACLAND NURSING HOME, OXFORD, *Nov.* 13, 1908

Mrs. Rollings and I are comfortably settled into this Nursing Home, waiting for a doctor from London to make an examination. I inform the doctor that, as a specialist is going to examine me, he is sure to find what he is looking for, and of course I shall have to have an operation of what he finds. They all say it will relieve me entirely, but I doubt it. However, by the time this reaches thee it will all be settled and done with. If I *should* die, which of course is always possible, what I would like would be to be cremated, and no funeral, and no weeping relatives to gather around my bed. Thee must not think of coming over no matter what happens. I do not expect to make an edifying death-bed, and I would far rather no one should " gather around " it.

Nov. 22, 1908

Thy loving letter came this morning and was a joy to my heart. I cannot understand how thee *can* love me so much, but I am *very* happy that thee does, and I shall keep it at the back of my mind, as a downright comfort and stand-by that, if I need thee, thee will really and truly be glad to come. Had I been going to have a severe operation I certainly should have wanted thee, but I have put my foot down about that, and do not intend at my age, to pay any man £100 to cut me up.

I must wait with very joyful anticipations for the happy call to my home in Heaven, only hoping and praying it may come before I get too old and decrepit to be any longer lovable. My one greatest of all alleviations is in my children and grandchildren. When I think of the joy I have had all my life in you, I feel struck with wonder that such joys *can* exist in a world like this. In looking over my old papers I came across a love letter I wrote thee for thy 19th birthday, and it brought back with great vividness the delight I had in thy girlhood, and the continuing delight of all thy womanhood, even although I could not always approve of all thee did. I put it in an envelope to send thee, and now I am not sure whether I sent it or not, although I cannot find it. If I sent it I hope it has made thee happy, as thy letter has made me. May God watch between us, my precious daughter, and keep our mutual love bright to the end !

To her daughter, Mary Berenson

Aet. 76.

IFFLEY, *Nov.* 26, 1908

This is the first Christmas for twenty-one years that I have not had the children to cater for, and I feel quite lost without them. What a joy and delight they have been to me ! Between you, thee and them,—you have given me forty years of happy interests, and with all my heart I thank you. Forty years is a good stretch of life, when you come to think of it ; and I daresay, before I am done, it will mount up to forty-five. I am already beginning to look forward to your home-coming ; and it almost reconciles me to going on living, if I may feel that this may be your home for all the years that lie before me.

Now that the girls are grown up, I shall not take any responsibility about them any more, and they may come and go as they please, and I will not worry if they are out late on the river, or spoil all their clothes ! I shall dismiss them from the caretaking side of my mind, and keep them simply and solely for the joy and delight of my pleasure-taking side. And when I think of the pure delight of having you all making this your home, I feel rather glad you have not got any other English home to entice you away from me. I am sure you could get along with Logan, for he is most easy and comfortable to live with when you once understand his little peculiarities.

I think the last book I write must be called " The Secrets of the Bladder ", and the motto on the title page shall be " For ways that are dark and tricks that are vain, consider the Bladder " !

The minute anything turns up that is likely to add to my comfort, you may all rest assured I will have it, no matter what it costs. I consider it is my *first* duty in life to make myself as comfortable as is possible, so you may make all your minds easy on that score. This is *my* interpretation of the text, " He giveth us richly all things to enjoy."

To her daughter, Mary Berenson

Aet. 77.

IFFLEY, *July* 18, 1909

I certainly am not good for much, and I cannot help wondering why I should be left to cumber the ground, or why any old people are. If it was only arranged for us to die off automatically say at 70, how much suffering and how much money could be saved, and how much pleasanter memories we would leave behind us ! I am thankful you are none of you here to worry over my attack of pain, for I cannot bear anyone near me. I really think if a company of angels from Heaven should come to visit me, I would lock the door on them !

The plan must wait awhile, until I am dead anyhow. I am afraid all my—— (Here I went unexpectedly to sleep, and what I was afraid of I cannot imagine, and now I must close for the post.)

To her daughter, Mary Berenson

Aet. 77.

October 4, 1909

I told Logan and Ray at dinner last night with great glee that sometimes I have a lovely whizzing or buzzing in my head that I *hope* means apoplexy, and it quite heartens me to think that the time may be shorter than I fear.

To her daughter, Mary Berenson

Aet. 77.

IFFLEY, *Nov.* 11, 1909

I am enclosing an interesting " find " I came across in a box of tracts the other day. It is a little life of me by Frances Willard, and it surprised me very much to find what a nice person I was ! I really had no idea of it ! Whether true or not, it is what Frances thought of me, and to look like that sort of person in her eyes I feel to be a decided feather in my cap. Thee has no idea how set up I am in my own opinion !

I asked Ray if she knew what falling in love means. She said, " Yes, it means feeling what you feel for your friends, only more so." But that does not seem to me adequate. How would *thee* define it ? And to me " love at first sight " is an unknown and unexplored region. I cannot conceive of it.

Perhaps your trip to Rome will break the spell of poor B. B.'s rage at the things that go wrong at I Tatti. I really cannot blame him, for from all thy accounts it must be more than human nature can be expected to bear. In comparison our lives seem like peaceful unruffled mountain lakes. Only just at this moment there is a ruffle, as I have lost the Water Rates paper. (But now I have suddenly remembered where it is, so that ruffle is over.)

We have another worry too over Grace's cottage. The day after Grace left, a man and his wife came as tenants, who seemed all that was respectable, and who paid a month's rent in advance. We felt quite pleased. But they have turned out to be most disreputable. They keep an army of dogs and parrots, etc. on our carpets ; they are covering all our nice clean walls with filth ; they won't pay any more rent ; they quarrel like cats and dogs ; and they won't go out, though Logan has given them notice.

They call Logan a " female worm ", because he is so gentlemanly in his methods, I suppose, and he, poor fellow, is powerless, and of course I am too. Thee says, and most truly, that all this grapple to live cannot be the end-all and be-all of our sojourn in this world. If it were, suicide would be a virtue as well as an enormous privilege. But as soon as one sees that the whole thing is part of the process of our evolution into the likeness and image of God, it becomes glorified ; and we can embrace every pang and every worry as most valuable gifts and blessings.

To her daughter, Mary Berenson

Aet. 77.

IFFLEY, *Dec.* 5, 1909

I am all alone, but I have in my bladder one faithful companion who never leaves me for five minutes at a time, and whose demands are incessant—my Mistress of Ceremonies ; so I cannot be lonely. I have had plenty of time to think over thy letter, with much of which I heartily agree, and that is that if one wants to have a home the woman must make it. It is manifest that this is our share in the family arrangement, and that we must put our best energies into it.

But then it is also manifest that we must not undertake a style of housekeeping that is not to *our* taste, and to which *our* capabilities are not equal, for we shall be sure to make a failure of it, and if B. B. goes on worrying about your house as he has been doing, he will end in an asylum, I am afraid. If one believed in Black Magic, one would think Mrs. Ross must be directing it against you. Ask her if she believes in it, and, if she does, whether she ever exercises it, and see what she says.

I cannot comprehend that " last word " in Art, if the picture thee drew is a sample. There is not one hint of Art in it to my mind. B. B. has got up so high that I think he must have fallen backwards and doesn't know it. Do tell me soberly whether that woodenlike creature in the Chinese book is *really* considered good Art. It seems incredible to me. And Matisse, too, the man who, when he paints a side face, puts an eye in the cheek, so as to have two eyes—does B. B. really consider that Art ? Logan says Roger Fry does !

To her daughter, Mary Berenson

Aet. 77.

IFFLEY, *Dec.* 14, 1909

Men are by nature unreasonable and have to be cajoled. They cannot be driven but must be coaxed. One feels undignified in descending to such methods, and yet I feel sure it is the best way. From the fact of their position of Lordship, encouraged at first by the wife's self-abnegation, they get to a place where they *have* to be managed ; and the wives I have known who have made a success of marriage have always been women to pet and coax their husbands. No man can resist petting and coaxing.

It is one of my uncomfortable days, and I cannot write much. I do not believe there is such an all-absorbing occupation to be found anywhere as the one I am kept busy with, namely waiting on my " Mistress of Ceremonies ". There is not a single five minutes in the day when she is not making some demand or other ; and she is only quiet when I fall asleep for two or three hours in my chair at night. It really does seem a ridiculous occupation for a woman with brains !

It really is amazing how your " Woes " continue to be unending ! It must be intended to teach you the unalterable imperfection of all human things ; and I believe in the end you will have to settle down to it, and consent to stop short of perfection. I long ago had to do this, and it has produced such a feeling of being only a stranger and a pilgrim here, with my real home beyond, that it has relieved me immensely. Poor B. B. will just have to *settle down* to having things wrong, and then he will not mind, and it will not make much difference in the end.

Life, I find, is full of " settlings down ", and nothing really matters except one's own spirit, and one's health. But as long as you have " woes " to relate we *must* hear them, and shall never be tired of hearing. You have certainly had at least 150 by this time, or even 200. We go with thee step by step in all thy experiences, and daily letters are the principal excitements of our day. They are like a serial story in the morning paper.

This sentence expresses my Theology in a few words : " It is enough to know that God's responsibility is irrevocable, and His resources limitless." This covers the whole ground of my heresies. By-the-bye, when I say it is foolish to try to be pious when God only wants us to be happy, I mean of course by pious that side of religion that consists in emotions, and pious feelings, and religious performance. I do not mean being *good*. Good we must be, or we cannot be happy, but some of the very best people I know are not pious at all. They are just plain commonplace *good* ; and to be good is necessarily to be happy. There is no happiness in the world equal to the happiness of being good.

To her daughter, Mary Berenson

Aet. 77.

IFFLEY, *Jan.* 3, 1910

I am perfectly overwhelmed with Christmas and New Year's cards. I expect people think, " Oh, we must not forget the poor old lady," but the poor old lady wants to be neglected, if they only knew.

It does not do to know too much about the private

lives of our servants. Their whole standards are so entirely different from ours that I believe it is impossible for us to understand them. But God knows our frame and remembers we are but dust, and He must understand the different kinds of dust, one kind as well as another, and must judge accordingly. But the very thought of the cook hugging her beau in the kitchen irritates me so that I believe if she stayed on I should have nervous prostration.

I wish advertisements did not always seem such gospel truth to me. But I cannot seem able to believe that anyone would dare to *print* things that are untrue, even if they do not mind saying them.

I wonder if thee remembers the Chicken Pot-pies of America ? I have the tenderest memories of them, and I have always longed to try having one over here, but never had a chicken to waste on the experiment. However, as I happened to have one to-day that no one seems likely to want, I am having Mary try a recipe that I have concocted out of an American Cookery book and out of my memory combined, and for my dinner this evening I shall try the result. When I read out the recipe to Mary she smiled quite unctuously and said, " That *does* sound good," so I have hopes. I am not having any tea !

To her daughter, Mary Berenson
Aet. 78.

IFFLEY, *March* 1, 1910

Never shall I forget the wave of enthusiasm that swept over me when, in a London Hotel, I read the reports that were sent to me from America of the Women's Temperance Crusade. I remember I began to read the accounts as I stood by the window looking out on the London streets, and I became so absorbed that London and all its sights was utterly forgotten, and I found myself marching in spirit with my American sisters ; and the first thing I knew I found myself sitting down hard in the nearest chair, and heard myself saying aloud in perfectly triumphant tones over and over, " I belong to those women ! I belong ! I belong ! " And so I did, from that moment, and no signing of my name or recording of my membership anywhere could make me more completely and utterly one of them. I wrote over to America at once and told them so, and from that moment it became the chief interest of my life.

The idea of arranging your furniture so as to necessitate knocking fresh holes in your walls, and upsetting your heating apparatus, does not appeal to me as being either fun or a proper woe. All my nearly eighty years of life I have made *my* furniture arrangements fit in with the existing arrangements of the rooms, and I have lived and flourished under it, and have been happy. How much you would be saved it you could only walk in *my* footsteps.

I don't want Ray to get an absolutely incurable disgust for falling in love, which after all has a great deal that is beautiful in it, and I cannot help hoping that she will herself experience a refined form of it. Sometime ! !

They think thee is deceived in thy cook and say she is like our gardener's wife, so plausible that she can twist you around her little finger. I could easily be deceived by Mrs. B. [the gardener's wife] if it was not that I have found her out in lies, and I know she cheats whenever she can. But even so, every time she comes to see me, I always believe, *while she is with me*, that she is the very salt of the earth.

To her granddaughter, Ray Costelloe

Aet. 78.

IFFLEY, *March* 22, 1910

I cannot help feeling that to be without any real faith in God, and without knowing of His love and care, is an irreparable loss to the soul, and to all the higher nature ; and opens the door to miseries and un-happiness that could not possibly enter into a heart that hides itself in the keeping of a loving God. Don't shut thyself out too determinedly against what long years of experience have taught me is by far the purest joy our hearts can hold. At least, darling Ray, keep an open mind, and listen to the still small voice of God that I am sure speaks to thy inner consciousness some-times and tries to draw thee to Himself. To His loving care I commit thee, and, even though thee may not yet thyself know Him, He will always surround thee with His love.

To her daughter, Mary Berenson

Aet. 78.

IFFLEY, *March* 25, 1910

Thy letter received this morning was lovely and long, and it was the only one I had to console me. I almost live on your dear letters. As I set forth in moving language to Ray and Karin, if I had not married I would not have had you, and then what would my old age have been ? Daughters are wonderful luxuries ! They are well worth a bad husband in my opinion ; at least mine are : I would have stood *any* kind of husband for the sake of having you !

I wrote to my praying friend that I thought it was only fair to tell her I was a little better, and that I knew no cause for it unless it was her prayers. But I added that she must restrain her prayers a little, as I did not want to be made *entirely* well and so lose my chance of going home to Heaven, which I hoped my illness was preparing the way for. I wonder how she will manage this dilemma.

Yes, all thee says about adjusting your minds to people, when circumstances seem to make it necessary to live with them, is profoundly true. Once you have really found out a person's incurable weaknesses you can *settle down* to them and cease to be troubled by them, and can see their virtues instead. It is a great secret to discover. To me it always comes by the way of religion. I say " Thy will be done " to God about a thing, and it no longer troubles me.

I do not mean, in a case like Lucy's for instance, that it is the will of God that she should be such an unmitigated goose, and that I must say " Thy will be done " to that, but I do mean that, when it seems necessary that a goose should live with me, I can accept the infliction of her presence as the will of God, and should say " Thy will be done " to such infliction. By whatever process one works, it is everlastingly true, as Fénelon says, " I conquered my trial by submitting to it." But I must say I sympathise with you from the bottom of my heart for the amount of boring company you have ; and you do not seem to have hit upon any way to relieve yourselves.

It is pure waste and awfully fatiguing to spend days like the one described in thy letter that came this morning. If I had not had the excuse of invalidism to save me from the society around here I think I should have lost my reason, and I do not see how you *can* stand it. Could you not sometimes excuse yourselves ? Could you not adopt the fashionable way of saying " Not at home ", or whatever the Italian substitute is for that, and only see the people you invite or who have asked beforehand for interviews ? But no doubt self-preservation will sooner or later force you to find some relief.

I have had quite a lesson lately on how little we really know what is good for us. The Donnington Trustees had sold some trees to a lumber merchant, and among them two trees that bordered my view of the river and the bridge over which Alys comes to see me. I thought these two trees were indispensable to the beauty of my outlook out of my big window in my sitting-room, and I moved Heaven and earth to prevent their being cut down, and made poor Logan do the same. But everybody concerned was so cantankerous, and the lumber man was so bullying that finally I gave up in despair, and decided to let them go without any further resistance, and they were cut down, and I felt like a martyr. But lo and behold a perfectly lovely view of the river was opened out to me, and I would not have them put back for anything.

To her daughter, Mary Berenson

Aet. 78.

IFFLEY, *April* 13, 1910

Our lawn is ablaze with daffodils, and our grass is like a velvet pile carpet, and the river, as seen through my newly opened space, looks lovely. I feel far more vividly than I did before the opening was cut (against which I so sorely rebelled), that our place is really on the river banks. The migratory birds are all coming back, and the whole air is full of their singing. I can hardly imagine what your country must be like with no singing of birds. We are now watching for the Cuckoo and the Nightingale, which rumour declares have been heard in different parts of the country, but we have no signs of them yet.—But enough of birds, although they are certainly a contrast to " woes ". My present " woe " is that I *cannot* get a comfortable cushion to sit on. I have tried everything, and have spent pounds in my experiments, but it has all been of no use. I sit down on everything like a heavy block of granite, and no springs or downy pillows can withstand the load.

I have never expected Alys to stay permanently at Bagley Wood and she says she will make a point of coming down for every weekend. But people do sometimes die at my age, and I have faint hopes that I shall be able to make my escape before I get lonely. A life spent literally in obeying the continual nagging of one's bladder and other indecent parts of one's nature can *not* be said to be particularly tempting, and thee must not be surprised that, dearly as I love you all, I still want to go. I *want* to go, but alas ! I see no signs of any chance, so I must possess my soul in patience. But it would be nice if I could only cut all the knots by skipping off to Heaven.

To her daughter, Mary Berenson

Aet. 78.

IFFLEY, *June* 8, 1910

Poor dear B. B. I can sympathise with him, for the two days of my attack I felt cross enough to insult an angel from Heaven. It is the greatest comfort to remember that somewhere it says of God " He knoweth our frame and remembereth that we are dust." And, since this of course is an incontrovertible fact, it follows that He does not expect much of us, and must be always ready with excuses. I can't tell how often I think of this when I find myself unable to come up to any of the usually expected conventionalities of piety, and am absolutely swallowed up by my bladder and its unintermitted requirements. I just say to Him, " You understand. You remember I am dust," and then I feel entirely comfortable about myself. I wonder if B. B. could not do something like this, for he must hate being cross just as I hate not being pious.

It is a doleful day of thunder and lightning and pouring rain. Logan says it is good for the garden, but I am not a garden, and I do not like it. I can hardly see to write, and must call for the lamps although it is only 4 o'clock.

To her daughter, Mary Berenson

Aet. 78.

IFFLEY, *Sept.* 19, 1910

Just now I am greatly exercised about the birds. I have a table with crumbs set just inside my open window, and I was beginning to entice the Tits and the darling Robin Redbreasts to come in and feed, to my great pleasure ; when behold the ugly greedy sparrows have come in crowds, and have driven the others entirely away. It is most provoking. There they come, the gluttons.

Is the little Chapel still at I Tatti ? I hope so, for in that Chapel I had one of my " openings " in regard to all the Catholic ceremonies, that took away forever my prejudices, and made me feel that it was a *fact* that we are all one in God. Such openings are tremendously enlightening. I love to have them. It is not that one changes one's own idea of what is best in religion, but only that one sees that exactly opposite ideas may be quite as honest as one's own, and need not necessarily have bad or mean motives behind them.

But I really must stop sermonising, as old heads never did and never will fit on younger shoulders. Mrs. Creighton is going to make a speech somewhere on how to grow old gracefully, and she was talking to a friend about it and asking for hints. The friend replied that in her opinion the whole philosophy of old age could be expressed in a sentence composed of four words, and this sentence was, " Toady to the young." Pretty sound PHILOSOPHY I reckon.

To her daughter, Mary Berenson

Aet. 78.

IFFLEY, *Sept.* 28, 1910

" Toady to the young " must more and more be the motto of the mothers, after their children are grown up. I must take myself in hand more strictly ! ! But thee must always remember when I venture to give thee any advice that it is *only* advice, and does not carry any obligation on thy part to obey it ; and I do not feel wounded in my feelings if thee does not follow it.

Two more darling Redbreasts have just taken lovely baths in the bowl outside my window. It is too sweet to see them. I fear in all thy grandeur thee has no place where thee can see such homely sights.

My callers were Christian Scientists who come periodically to visit me, hoping, I think, to convert me. But I am too old a bird for their bait, thus far.

I enclose Karin's speech on Compulsory Military Service. It is very good as far as it goes. But the surprising thing is that the child had any ideas at all on the subject. I do not believe I could have written anything so good at her age. England does make you think on public questions. In my girlhood we did not know there were any public questions, and would have

Q

as soon made speeches against the Ten Commandments, as against any Government Bill.

Ray and Karin are granddaughters to be proud of, and, as I tell them, I do not hesitate to indulge in that feeling whenever I think of them, which I must say is pretty often. I like to think that we have at least given them happy childhoods ; and, as grandpa Whitall used to say, if people have happy childhoods tucked under their jackets they will have a storehouse of happiness to last them all their lives. It gets them into the *habit* of happiness, which is a great thing.

Alas ! Ray went to her meeting looking like a factory girl ; but I said nothing, as I must not let myself get into the way of nagging her about her clothes, although I am sorely tempted sometimes. She *is* so pretty that it seems a shame to spoil it with shabby clothes.

It rejoices my heart that thee can say that B. B. is such a real comrade. It is hard for me to believe that any husband and wife are really happy together. And to have thee say you are is an unspeakable comfort.

To her daughter, Mary Berenson

IFFLEY, *Nov.* 8, 1910

To-day is a day full of events—

(1) It is B. B.'s home-coming.

(2) It was Crippen's death day (but that has been put off to the 23rd).

(3) It is the election day in America, when the question of Democracy versus Republicanism is to be settled.

(4) It is the meeting of " Congregation " in Oxford to discuss and decide on Lord Curzon's plans of reform for the University.

(5) Ray overcame her dislike of shopping so far as to buy herself a waterproof coat, as her own is in shreds.

Nov. 10, 1910

I am delighted thee is having thy picture taken to hang up in my chamber of horrors. But *my* day is passed for having a picture taken. I look too thin and haggard, and not at all like the cheerful contented individual I really am. I do not want you to remember me as I look now, but as I looked in the enclosed card, which to my mind was my prime. Anybody would think, to look at my haggard face now, that I had not a speck of religion anywhere about me.

The Dr. asked to feel my pulse. " It could not be better," was his verdict, and when he went out he said to Mrs. Rollings, " Well Mrs. Smith is as right as rain." So there is evidently no hope of escape for me yet, I am sorry to say. The only encouraging symptom I have is that I am all the time getting thinner and thinner, and I may perhaps fade away sometime.

To her daughter, Mary Berenson
Aet. 78.

IFFLEY, *Dec.* 5, 1910

Elections are still our only interest. Alys and Logan fairly devour the papers, and the only question anybody asks anybody is—How do you think it is going ? and nobody can guess. At the bottom *I* fear it is going Tory, but that may be because my servants keep me riled with their Toryism !

It looks rather hopeful, but we are very anxious.

There is hardly any chance of a fair election in England, owing to the power of the Landlords, and the arbitrary way they exercise it. But I understand why they do, for my servants are Tories, and I simply *hate* them, and if it would not inconvenience me too much, I would turn them out at once! So what can I say?

If B. B. does not like Aristea's cooking there is nothing for thee to do but to change it. I myself would not think of keeping a cook whose cookery even Logan disliked. You *have* to please men with the cookery, or they will be worse than bears with sore heads. That is the experience of a woman nearly 79 years old, who does not believe in humouring men too much, but who knows in cooking you HAVE to!

And I sit in my wheeled chair and look on at you all in your different lives and interests, and love to know every little detail because, as thee says, it is *you*. But I think, apart from its being thee, thy "woes" are tremendously interesting to themselves, and I am ashamed to say we do like hearing of them. Also it all seems more like a novel than anything else in our experiences, and we get quite excited when thy letters come, and wonder what has happened now.

To her daughter, Mary Berenson

Aet. 78.

IFFLEY, *Dec.* 10, 1910

I think English politics are perfectly demoralising. I feel all demoralised myself, and would like to give some Tory a good shaking, especially my servants. And I have to pretend they are all right! Mrs. Rollings is worse than ever I am. I do not know what I *should* do if she was a Tory.

It makes life a different thing when people enjoy

the things you provide, and *say so*, and to act upon this maxim I will tell thee now that thy daily letters are one of the brightest spots in my life. I delight in every word, and although I hate the woes, I love to hear about them.

Dec. 18, 1910

Karin's letter gives a delightful impression of I Tatti, in spite of all the woes. Only I am afraid you are *too* luxurious, and poor old Court Place will seem very homely in comparison. But, at any rate, if we have no great luxuries, we do not have any great woes, and things go smoothly without electric lights, and without corridors hung with Old Masters.

To her daughter, Mary Berenson

Aet. 79.

IFFLEY, *Feb.* 7, 1911

This is my 79th birthday, but I wish it was my 89th as I should then be so much nearer my happy escape. But alas, I think I am really better than on my last birthday. Still this is a comfort in one way, as it means a good deal less discomfort physically.

The Marchese Visconti-Venosta [1] came in to tea yesterday. He told us that he had seen your new

[1] The son of Emilio, Marchese Visconti-Venosta, a follower of Mazzini, and at one time a member of the Italian foreign ministry under Cavour, whose grandniece he married. Of the son, Logan Pearsall Smith used to tell how, when he first came to Oxford, he was made drunk at an undergraduate party. Next morning this great-grand-nephew of Cavour came to himself, and, reflecting on the manners of his own country, thought, "I'm done for! I shall have to leave Oxford at once, leave England!" He was much surprised and relieved to find that his mishap was looked on in the England of that day more as an accomplishment than a degradation.

Frescoes, and they were perfect monstrosities, tomato-red naked women set in bright blue landscapes ! He is working 8 hours a day, but finds the cottage he has taken in Iffley so low that he cannot walk up straight inside it, and I should think it would be rather forlorn. But he said he had to get away from the College, as the set he got into never studied, but spent their time going to Hunts, and driving around in Drags, and getting drunk every night. It is exactly what I believed of the Colleges ; but how the Dons can allow it is beyond me.

To her daughter, Alys Russell
Aet. 79.

IFFLEY, *Feb.* 8, 1911

I *shall* be glad if thy bag and the down quilt make thy bed more comfortable. And they have helped me to find such a nice thing about God that I had never thought of before, and it was this—that if I enjoyed giving things to my children a thousand times more than keeping them for myself, so of course must He.

To her granddaughter, Karin Costelloe
Aet. 79.

IFFLEY, *Mar.* 9, 1911

My darling young woman, I am trying to realise that my fat curly-headed baby has really and truly become a young woman 22 years old, who is quite old enough to be married, and who no doubt has all the good sense necessary to manage all her own affairs, and to help to manage other people's as well, if they want thee to. I wonder what will follow later on. Love affairs, I fear me, and, who knows, marriage perhaps, and housekeeping, and servants to manage or be managed by, and perhaps the *bliss of babies*. For this last I shall envy thee, if it ever comes, but for all the rest thee shall have my deepest sympathy !

Well, I *might* give thee pages of good advice, but I expect it is wiser to let thee advise thyself, and I am sure of one thing and that is, that, whatever happens, thy heart and thy will are all right, and thee is sure to come out something splendid through it all. God bless thee, my darling, and make thee to know the truth that surely lies behind all the " mad philosophies " that are filling thy horizon at present. To cheer thee up in the midst of thy great responsibilities I have sent thee piles of good things to eat.

To her daughter Mary and granddaughters

Aet. 79.

IFFLEY, *Mar.* 25, 1911

I picture various contingencies as you drove off [to Cambridge], principally a break-down after dark in a lonely bit of the road, miles from everywhere, and Aunty Loo [1] and Ray struggling in vain to escape from the mountains of luggage.

To her daughter, Mary Berenson

Aet. 79.

IFFLEY, *March* 30, 1911

I have been out in my chair down to the Lodge to see to the planting on the mound there of some plants I bought in a weak moment, and when I got them had

---

[1] Her daughter, Alys Russell.

no idea what they were or where to put them. I simply cannot resist the Florists' lists, and I am free to confess that I act like a fool over them. They are the most dreadful snares, and tell such marvellous tales of plants that read as if they must be plants from Paradise. And again, in spite of all my past experience, I am simply making out a new list! And I have no idea where I shall plant them. Could there be greater folly?

March 31, 1911

I have had my last bout with the Flower lists this morning. They littered my table beyond words, and whenever I laid eyes on them the passion seized me, and thousands of rare and marvellous plants clamoured to be sent for. I made out about a dozen lists, and then resolutely put every Catalogue away in one of my Pedestal drawers, and shut it up with a bang, and have vowed not to open it again until next spring, and at last my mind feels at rest. I almost think I shall put my lists in their envelopes into the drawers with the Florist's books, and give up all thoughts of flowers that I cannot plant for want of places for them. It certainly would be wiser. But wisdom flies when Florists' lists appear ; I really have to hide them away or I should spend a fortune on them.

I do not think it is any kindness to old people to let them be spectacles to their friends, and, when I become a spectacle I lay it upon the consciences of my children to keep me in seclusion. Logan says it amuses Sir W. to go about and pay visits. I do not believe it. At any rate it will not amuse *me*, and I refuse to have anyone think it. Please make a note of this.

To her daughter, Mary Berenson

Aet. 79.

IFFLEY, *April* 19, 1911

I often wonder whether there is not an unwritten natural law which says " The more sentiment the less reality," for somehow it seems to work out that way very often.   A display of sentiment on the part of the Bishops lately has disgusted me.   They are having some sort of ceremonial connected with the coronation of the new King, and one of the Bishops in a most unctuous voice and manner gave an eulogy of the late King's private life, declaring he was one of the most noble and beautiful characters that England had ever known, and a pattern to all his subjects, etc. etc. Now that Bishop *must* have known all about the King's private life, and yet he could stand up there and tell such lies to God !   He even went so far as to offer public Thanksgiving to the Almighty for blessing England with such a King !   What are Bishops made of, that they can do such blasphemous things ?   I confess it has given me a great set-back about Bishops.

To her daughter, Mary Berenson

Aet. 79.

IFFLEY, *April* 20, 1911

When Logan gets to thee on Saturday, I want thee to notice his cough, without saying anything unless he asks thee.   (Do not let him know I have written.) He has had it now for months, and I think it grows worse.   But when I speak of it, he always says, " Oh, it is nothing.   Alys always has a cough all winter, and it does not hurt her, and why should I worry ? "   Now, *does* thee have a cough all winter, and does it pass off in the summer ? If he asks thee, be sure thee tells him the truth, (and tell me also) ; and tell him what thee does for it. But as long as he has this idea about thee, he will not do a thing. If he doesn't introduce the subject himself thee had better, if thee hears him coughing, so as to settle the matter.

Our garden is a perfect show with the daffodils, and primroses, and blue forget-me-nots and early tulips. Logan took me round this morning in my wheeled chair. It is too lovely for words. And *such* a heavenly day ! We are certainly being repaid for all those bleak winter days up to the 12th.

The clergyman and his wife have gone off for a three weeks holiday, and they have given me their canary to take care of, and their silver. Jessie takes care of the former, and the latter I have tucked under Logan's bed and said nothing. The canary's song is very disappointing. It is only a sort of harsh whistle.

To her friends

Aet. 79.

IFFLEY, *April* 28, 1911

I felt a great desire, during the season of Christmas and New Year's greetings, to send one myself to all the friends whom I love so much, but, owing to my difficulty in writing, it seemed impossible. In one of my wakeful hours at night, however, on the first day of the New Year, it suddenly came to me that I might send a circular greeting for 1911 to all of you, which would embody the substance of what I would love to say to each one individually, had I but the strength to do so.

I expect that first of all some of you may want to know just how I am, and what are my surroundings and my life. I am living with my son and my two granddaughters in a beautiful home on the banks of the Thames, not far from Oxford, with frequent visits from my daughter Mary from Italy, and at least a weekly visit from my daughter Alys, now living at Cambridge. I could not ask for a lovelier refuge in which to pass the last years of my life, nor for better company.

I am, as no doubt you all know, very much of an invalid, and am obliged to sit in a wheeled chair, both day and night, as my many infirmities prevent me from much lying in bed. But I am very comfortable in my chair, and get plenty of sleep. I cannot either read or write much, and am often not well enough to see my friends. In fact I have very little energy for anything, and am not even able to go on with a half finished book that I was in the midst of writing when I was taken ill. My old activities have all had to be laid aside, and I am only waiting and longing for the blessed call to my heavenly home. But I am glad to tell you that I am very happy and contented in my narrow life, and with my lessening capabilities, and can say, " Thy will be done " to my Divine Master from the very bottom of my heart.

I knew once an old coloured aunty who had been very active in Mission Work for many years, but was at last laid aside from it all by a severe cough that racked her day and night. One might think she would have been unhappy at being so set aside, but on the contrary she was always bright and cheerful. A friend who had known her in her days of activity, asked her how she was able to be so happy. " Why, honey," she replied, " in course, I'se happy. Once the Lord used to say to me, ' Nancy, come here and do this,' or ' Nancy, go there and do that ' ; and I knew His will was good, and I went and did what He said, and in course I was happy. And now He says, ' Nancy, lie here and cough,' and I know His will is good, and I lies here and coughs, and am just as happy." And in my measure I feel as Nancy did. Once my Divine Master sent me on His errands, and I knew His will was good, and was happy in trying to do it. And now He has shut me up to an invalid life, and tells me to sit in my wheeled chair, and to be content to let others do His errands and carry on His work, and I know His will is good just the same, and am happy in trying to accept it. . . .

Nancy and I . . . are rich in nothing of our own, but rich beyond words in the wisdom and goodness and love of our God. " Thou, oh God, art all we want, more than all in Thee we find." This God is our God, and He is enough !

This is my greeting for 1911 ; and, since it is so late, a Birthday greeting as well, as I was 79 a few days ago.

May all to whom I send this message say Amen and Amen !

INDEX

(*Note :* The nature of kinship with Mrs. Pearsall Smith is inserted in brackets after names of members of the family.)

229

Printed in Great Britain by Butler & Tanner Ltd., Frome and London